Trotsky's Diary in Exile

1935

Trotsky's Diary in Exile

1935

Translated from the Russian by
Elena Zarudnaya

With a Foreword by
Jean van Heijenoort

HARVARD UNIVERSITY PRESS
Cambridge, Massachusetts, and London, England
1976

Library of Congress Catalog Card Number 75–42972

ISBN 0–674–91006–0

Printed in the United States of America

Foreword by Jean van Heijenoort

Leon Trotsky was expelled from Russia at the beginning of 1929. He arrived in Istanbul, with his wife, Natalia, and his elder son, Liova, on 12 February 1929. Except for a four-week trip to Copenhagen at the end of 1932, he was in Turkey till 17 July 1933. This period of his life was relatively stable; there were, in particular, no difficulties with the Turkish authorities. True enough, there were misfortunes. The house in which he lived in Prinkipo burned down at 2 A.M. in the night between 28 February and 1 March 1931; some of his archives and manuscripts were destroyed, and his work was disorganized for a few weeks. His older daughter, Zinaida, killed herself in Berlin on 5 January 1933. And, on the political plane, there was, of course, the rise of Nazism in Germany, with Hitler becoming Chancellor on 30 January 1933. But the years in Turkey were, for Trotsky, very productive years. There he wrote two of his major works, *My Life* and *The History of the Russian Revolution*, plus several lesser books, quite a few pamphlets, and numerous articles — all that while conducting an abundant correspondence.

Trotsky left Turkey for France on 17 July 1933. He had been granted a visa by the Daladier government. There were no explicit restrictions in the visa; but, since there was a great deal of uncertainty about relations with the French authorities, it was decided to settle quite far from Paris. So on 25 July Trotsky came to a villa in Saint-Palais, near

Royan, on the Atlantic coast. August was a month of great activity. After the collapse of the Socialist and Communist parties in Germany, Trotsky had called for the formation of a new International, and, during this month of August 1933, there was in Saint-Palais a constant flow of visitors: members of Trotskyite groups or leaders of various groups that had broken from the Second or Third International. There were long talks and discussions, and all that was quite a change from the isolation in Prinkipo, where there would be a visitor, perhaps, every second or third month. In September Trotsky's health deteriorated. There were now winds and storms on the Atlantic coast. Natalia had left for a few weeks in Paris. After the excitement and tension of the political discussions during August, a reaction set in. Trotsky would stay in bed for days, doing hardly any work other than reading his mail and dictating a few letters.

On 9 October he left Saint-Palais by car, with Natalia and Jean Meichler, a member of the French Trotskyite group (shot by the Germans during World War II). The trip took the travelers south, to the Pyrénées. They stayed mostly in Bagnères-de-Bigorre, with excursions in the surrounding country. Thus they came to visit Lourdes, and the reader will find below (entry of 29 April) comments by Trotsky on this visit.

During the sojourn in Saint-Palais there had been no difficulties at all with the French authorities. The *préfet* had been notified, of course, that Trotsky was residing in his *département*. But the large number of visitors, many of them aliens, during the month of August had not provoked any reaction on the part of the French authorities, which seems to indicate that there was no direct local police surveillance of the villa. Emboldened by this situation, Trotsky and those around him decided that he could settle much nearer Paris, and on 1 November 1933, back from the Pyrénées, he came to live in a villa in Barbizon, some thirty miles southeast of Paris, at the verge of the Fontainebleau forest. The *Sûreté nationale* had given its consent, but the arrangement was somewhat conspiratorial. The local authorities, the *maire* in particular, had not been notified of Trotsky's presence in Barbizon. The only visitors to the villa were Liova (now living in Paris), Jeanne Martin, Henri and Raymond Molinier. Living in the house were, with Trotsky and Natalia, Rudolf Klement, Sara Weber (till the end of January 1934), Gabrielle Brausch, and myself. Nobody, in the quiet small town of Barbizon, suspected that the erect old man that they would see certain afternoons strolling in their streets was Trotsky.

Once settled in Barbizon, Trotsky started to work regularly again. After having hesitated between various projects for a new book, he had decided to write a biography of Lenin. Liova would bring him abundant materials drawn from libraries in Paris, and these began to be organized by chapters, in folders marked with a capital Cyrillic L in blue pencil. There was also a renewed flow of articles on current political events, plus, of course, the correspondence.

Soon there were trips to Paris. Every second or third Sunday, Trotsky would go to Paris to meet members of Trotskyite groups or left Socialists. These meetings would take place in various apartments that were frequently changed.

In the middle of April an incident occurred. One evening Rudolf Klement was returning from Paris to Barbizon on a motor bike on the Fontainebleau highway. His headlight went dead and he was soon stopped by two *gendarmes*. They found a young fellow speaking French with a heavy German accent, loaded with revolutionary publications, his pockets full of letters from all over the world, and unable to explain clearly who he was and where he was going. They arrested him, and that was the beginning of an *affaire* that was to unsettle Trotsky's life. It is possible that, at that time, the *gendarmerie* was already discreetly watching the villa. The inhabitants of the villa were strange enough to have provoked gossip in the then very sedate little town of Barbizon.

Shortly after that incident Liova came to Barbizon and drove away with Trotsky and Natalia; he took them to a villa in Lagny, east of Paris. A few days later Trotsky left for Chamonix by car with Jean Meichler. The French authorities would no longer tolerate his presence near Paris. Between 10 May and 28 May he stayed incognito, in a *pension de famille,* with Natalia and myself, in La Tronche, near Grenoble. Meanwhile, Henri Molinier was negotiating a new arrangement with the French authorities in Paris. There had been tumultuous political events in France. A proto-facist demonstration on the Place de la Concorde on 6 February 1934 had provoked a general strike on 12 February, and the center-left government of Daladier had been replaced by the center-right government of Doumergue. Henri Molinier's negotiations with the French authorities were difficult. There was talk of sending Trotsky to Madagascar. The Turkish government, discreetly approached, indicated that it did not care to have Trotsky back in Turkey. It was really the planet without a visa.

Not able to get rid of Trotsky, the French government agreed to a temporary arrangement whereby he could stay in France, but far from Paris and under constant police surveillance. So in June 1934 Trotsky lived in Saint-Pierre-de-Chartreuse, a small mountain village in the Alps, with

Natalia, Raymond Molinier, and Vera Lanis. Trotsky and Natalia had been provided by the *Sûreté nationale* with identification papers — carrying fictitious names and data. But the situation was precarious and in fact did not last long. There was an incident with the *préfet,* which Trotsky relates (entry of 8 May).

At about that time I went to visit Maurice Dommanget, in the village of the Oise *département* where he was a schoolteacher. Dommanget was a leader of the trade union of *instituteurs*, and I asked him if he knew of a schoolteacher who could shelter Trotsky in conditions that would be acceptable to the French authorities. Shortly thereafter, Dommanget let me know that he had found somebody, Laurent Beau, an *instituteur* in Domène, a small town ten miles north of Grenoble. Beau had a three-story house, surrounded by a large garden, on the *route de Savoie,* one or two miles outside of town. That was an ideal location. Beau was not a Trotskyite; he was a member of the leftist schoolteachers' union, and he was ready to rent part of the house to Trotsky.

Trotsky, Natalia, and I arrived in Domène shortly before mid-July 1934. The first arrangements were makeshift. There was no question of having a Russian typist, and Trotsky took to writing in longhand. For meals, Natalia would cook for Trotsky and herself, partly helped by Madame Beau. I would at times do the shopping, and most of the time I would eat out, to lighten the burden. All that was not very satisfactory. An *inspecteur* of the *Sûreté nationale,* Gagneux, was living in Domène, and he was keeping an eye on the house.

In the back of the house there were no neighbors, and the garden rose directly into the foothills of the Alps. There

Trotsky and Natalia could go for walks, totally undisturbed. Sometimes, in the evening, Beau would take us in his small car for a half-hour or an hour's ride in the countryside, without stops. Trotsky and Natalia would sit in the back, I would be next to Beau. The conversation with Beau was meager.

There was a small Trotskyite group in Grenoble, and one of its members, Alexis Bardin, had been informed of Trotsky's presence in Domène. He and his wife, Violette, became regular visitors to the house; there were conversations on local politics in Grenoble, and the reader will find below echoes of this interest of Trotsky's.

France was entering a tumultuous political time, and there was a lot to be done in the Trotskyite group in Paris; it was soon decided that I should share my time between Domène and Paris. I would stay three or four weeks in Paris, then go to Domène for two or three weeks, and so on. The arrangement was not rigid, of course, but depended on the necessities of the day. With time I came to spend more and more time in Domène. I was there in October and November, to translate the first part of *Whither France?* I was translating the manuscript as Trotsky was writing it in longhand. The pamphlet was an analysis of the political situation in France and, of course, it could not be published then under Trotsky's name. My translation was designed so as to obliterate the most obvious marks of his style. The text was published as written by the leadership of the French Trotskyite group. The Russian manuscript was to be saved, nevertheless. Natalia sewed it in the lining of my jacket when I was about to go back to Paris. I was in Domène during the month of January 1935, translating Trotsky's pamphlet on the Kirov assassination. In February and March

I was translating the second part of *Whither France?* It is at that time that Trotsky started his diary (7 February 1935).

By then the arrangement in the house had been somewhat modified. Trotsky and Natalia now had a complete floor to themselves; a new bathroom had been built there. Books had arrived from Paris and had been shelved in a corridor. But, precisely because the new setup had required some financial arrangements, the relations with the Beaus had deteriorated. The construction of the new bathroom had necessitated a relatively large sum (neither Trotsky nor Beau had much money), and there had been some haggling about it. Trotsky's remark at the end of the 12 February entry refers to this episode. His mention of "primitive accumulation" is certainly out of place and not even very good Marxist economics. Laurent Beau was receiving rent, but Trotsky was not an ordinary tenant and, in view of the political instability of France and Europe at that time, there was an element of risk, for himself and his family, in what Beau was doing.

A small group of visitors came to Domène. Liova, Jeanne Martin, Henri and Raymond Molinier came fairly regularly. Raymond Molinier once brought Marceau Pivert. Henryk Sneevliet and Pierre Naville came for political discussions. Once Yvan Craipeau came, but, because of Gagneux's surveillance, had to be hidden in the trunk of the car while going back through the town of Domène.

On 8 June 1935 I arrived from Paris in Domène with the news that the Norwegian government had granted a visa to Trotsky. We had to leave for Paris as soon as possible. In two days Natalia and I packed personal effects, some manuscripts, and a few books. We took the train for Paris in Grenoble in the evening of 10 June. Gagneux was with us. As we were to enter the railroad car, he drew my attention to the *préfet*, who, standing on another platform, was watching Trotsky's departure from his *département*. Trotsky and Natalia had a compartment to themselves and slept stretched on the seats. I stood at the door, in the corridor, and we arrived in Paris in the early morning. Trotsky and Natalia went for a few days to the apartment of Gérard Rosenthal, or rather of his father, a well-known Parisian doctor. There, during that short period, Trotsky met quite a few members of the French Trotskyite group. These few days are described in detail by Trotsky himself (entry of 20 June).

In the night of 13 to 14 June, we left Paris for Antwerp by train, Trotsky, Natalia, and I, together with Jean Rous. In Antwerp we met Jan Frankel, who had arrived from Prague; Rous went back to Paris, and in the evening of 15 June we sailed for Oslo, on the Norwegian steamship *Paris*. We arrived in Oslo on 18 June in the morning, and left immediately by car for Jevnaker, where we stayed for a few days in a *pension de famille*. On 23 June we settled in the house of Konrad Knudsen, in Honefoss, a small town some forty miles (as the crow flies) northwest of Oslo. Trotsky's diary dies out with a few entries in July and one in September.

The diary gives a vivid picture of Trotsky's interests and concerns. But, to one who was with him during that period and also, for comparison, before and after, the proportions between these various interests and concerns are not always the same in the diary as in reality. For example, a large part of Trotsky's time, even during the period covered by the diary, was taken up by the organizational problems of the various Trotskyite groups in about thirty countries. In practically each of these groups there was a struggle between two, three, or more factions, on personal or ideological grounds. Trotsky was always devoting a great deal of his time and energy to the factional fights, and this hardly comes to light in the diary.

One should also keep in mind the fact that the period covered by the diary was rather different from the other years of Trotsky's exile. Before, in Turkey, and after, in Mexico, he was free from petty police harassment; he was living in a large house that he had all to himself; there were around him three or four secretaries, sometimes also additional guards; he was able to invite journalists and give them statements whenever he wanted. So the reader should not forget that the diary was written under rather special conditions (one may wonder if it was these unusual conditions that provoked Trotsky to keep a diary).

Also, with all the afflictions and hardships of the period covered by the diary, one should not lose sight of the fact that Trotsky was a hard worker and a fecund writer. The list of his writings, of all kinds, during that period remains impressive. Even in the somber months of the spring of 1935, there was in his eyes, when he would bring me for translation a sheaf of pages covered with his neat handwriting, a gleam of satisfaction and optimism.

December 1975

PUBLISHER'S NOTE

Harvard University Press was permitted to publish the Diary of 1935 and the Testament of 1940 because the handwritten originals of these documents are part of the Trotsky Archive of Harvard University Library, which consists of his surviving papers since the Russian Revolution. The presence of these unique private documents in the Trotsky Archive, and the permission to publish them, were due to the author's widow, Natalia Ivanovna Sedova-Trotsky.

The Diary of 1935 is written in three notebooks. The first notebook is an ordinary school copybook of a kind used by French schoolboys. The paper is white and ruled; the cover is dark blue in color and made of stiff cardboard. This first notebook measures 8⅝ by 6⅞ inches. It contains pages 1–138 inclusive of the handwritten Diary. The second notebook is also an ordinary schoolboy's copybook, of the same dimensions as the first, but thinner and with a light blue and less stiff cardboard cover. It is ruled, like the first notebook (although it is interesting to note that Trotsky did not follow the lines in these notebooks, disregarding them almost completely). It contains pages 139–184 of the Diary; these pages do not completely fill the second notebook, about one-third of it being blank. These first two notebooks were bought in Grenoble. The third notebook is of a different type; it is a pad, with a yellowish brown soft paper cover and with pages of rather thin paper perforated at the top. It is not ruled. Its measurements are 10¾ by 8⅜ inches. It contains pages 185–203 (the last page) of the Diary, which takes up only about one-fifth of the notebook, the remaining four-fifths being blank. Trotsky pasted clippings from newspapers, letters, and various other kinds of printed and handwritten matter to the pages of his Diary, usually identifying the sources by writing directly on the clipping, or above it, in his own hand. Examples will be found among the illustrations of this book.

The Testament of 1940 is handwritten on ordinary office paper (Hammermill Bond) and is of course unruled. The parts of the Testament dated 27 February 1940 are written on three sheets of this paper, measuring 11 by 8½ inches. The postscript to the Testament, dated 3 March 1940, is written on a fourth sheet of the same paper; this fourth sheet has been trimmed to dimensions of 8⅜ by 7¾ inches.

CONTENTS

ILLUSTRATIONS

THE DIARY

February 1935

February 7, 1935

The diary is not a literary form I am especially fond of; at the moment I would prefer the daily newspaper. But there is none available . . . Cut off from political action, I am obliged to resort to such ersatz journalism as a private diary. At the beginning of the war, when I was confined in Switzerland, I kept a diary for a few weeks. Later, after being deported from France to Spain in 1916, I did so again. I think that is all. Now once again I have to resort to a political diary. Will it be for long? Perhaps months; in any case not years. Events must come to a head in one way or another and put an end to the diary — if it is not cut short even sooner by a surreptitious shot directed by an agent of . . . Stalin, Hitler, or their French friend-enemies.

Lassalle wrote once that he would gladly leave unwritten what he *knew* if only he could accomplish at least a part of what he felt able to *do*. Any revolutionary would feel the same way. But one has to take the situation as it is. For the very reason that it fell to my lot to take part in great events, my past now cuts me off from chances for action. I am reduced to interpreting events and trying to foresee their future course. At least this occupation is more satisfying than mere passive reading.

Here my contacts with life are almost entirely limited to the newspapers and partly to letters. It will not be surprising if my diary tends to take the form of a review of newspapers and periodicals. But it is not the world of the newspapermen as such that interests me, but the workings of the deeper social forces as they appear reflected in the crooked mirror of the press. However, I naturally am not committing myself in advance to this form. The advantage of a diary — alas, the only one — lies precisely in the fact that it leaves one free from any literary requirements or prescriptions.

* * *

February 8

It is hard to imagine a more painful occupation than reading Léon Blum. Although he is an educated and, in his way, intelligent man, he seems to have set himself the aim in life of uttering nothing but parlor trivialities and pretentious nonsense. The explanation for this is that he is a political has-been. Our whole epoch is not for him. His minuscule talents, suitable for parliamentary lobbying, seem wretched and paltry in the awesome whirlpool of our days.

In today's issue there is an article devoted to the anniversary of February 6th. Of course *"le fascisme n'a pas eu sa journée!"* But still, Flandin is far from being equal to the situation: *"les émeutiers fascistes se fortifient contre sa faiblesse."* Blum, the tower of strength, reproaches Flandin for his weakness. Blum presents Flandin with an ultimatum: *"Pour ou contre l'émeute fasciste!"* But Flandin is by no means obliged to choose. All his "strength" lies in the fact that he stands between *l'émeute fasciste* and *la défense ouvrière*. The weaker Blum and Cachin are, the nearer the resultant force approaches the fascists.

Stalin once delivered himself of an aphorism: Social Democracy and fascism are twins! Nowadays it is Social

Democracy and Stalinism — Blum and Cachin — that have become twins. They are doing everything in their power to ensure the victory of fascism.

In *L'Humanité* there is the same triumphant headline: *"Ils n'ont pas eu leur journée!"* It was the weak Flandin who provided this triumph for the mighty "United Front." The threat by the United Front to bring the workers out onto the Place de la Concorde, i.e., to expose the unarmed and unorganized masses to the guns and brass knuckles of militarized gangs, would have been criminal adventurism if it had been a serious threat in the first place. But it was mere *bluff* [in English], arranged in advance with the "weak" Flandin. In the good old days Victor Adler used to be a past master of such tactics, and where is his party now? Today's denunciations of Flandin both in *Popu* and in *Huma* are a mere cover-up for yesterday's agreement with him. These gentlemen think they can cheat history. They will only cheat themselves.

Meanwhile, *Le Temps* is fighting against corruption and the decline in morals.

February 9

Rakosi has been sentenced to hard labor for life. He behaved with revolutionary dignity — after several years in prison. In any case, it was certainly not the protests of *L'Humanité,* which hardly evoked any response, that saved him from execution. A much more important factor was the tone of the large metropolitan French press, beginning with *Le Temps.* That paper was "for" Rakosi against the Hungarian government, just as it had been "against" Zinoviev for Stalin's justice — in both cases, of course, out of "patriotic" considerations. And what other considerations might *Le Temps* have?

In the Zinoviev case, to be sure, there were also considerations of social conservatism: the Moscow correspondent of *Le Temps,* who evidently knows very well where to look for directives, stressed several times that Zinoviev, like all the oppositionists now being persecuted, stood to the *left* of the government and that therefore there was not the slightest basis for alarm. It is true that Rakosi stands to the left of Horthy — a great deal to the left, in fact — but in this case it is a matter of doing a small favor for the Kremlin. A disinterested one, we must assume?

* * *

The Ministry of the Interior has forbidden the workers' counterdemonstrations scheduled for February 10th. By demanding of the "weak" Flandin that he dissolve the fascist leagues, Cachin and Blum strengthen his hand against the workers' organizations. The machinery of neo-Bonapartism is evident. Cachin-Blum will of course revile Flandin in print — which benefits Flandin as much as it does them. At heart these gentlemen will rejoice at the ban against workers' demonstrations; everything will get back to normal, God willing, and they will be able to continue their useful function as oppositionists.

The number of strikers receiving assistance has meanwhile grown to 483,000. Blum sent Frossard to make a speech in the Chamber of Deputies on the question of the strikers. This is really addressed to the bourgeoisie and means "Don't get upset about the strikers. They are no threat to you. Just preserve the parliament and our liberties for us."

February 11

Despite their colorlessness, the memoirs of Röhm, the Chief of Staff of the S.A., who was subsequently killed by Hitler, give quite a clear picture of the self-assured vulgarity of that milieu. In Nazi "socialism" the psychological survivals of the "class reconciliation" of the trenches are still very important. "Barracks socialism," the expression that Martov and other Mensheviks used to apply to Bolshevism — without the slightest foundation — is fully applicable to the Nazis, at least to their recent past. In the figure of Röhm himself this barrack-room "brotherhood" is very organically connected with pederasty.

Nevertheless, this narrow-minded *Landsknecht,* who for lack of opportunity to fight for Germany was once willing to fight for Bolivia, has a naturalistic approach to people and things which enables him to make some very apt observations quite beyond the capacity of parlor socialists.

"Flammende Proteste und Massen-Versammlungen sind zur Erzeugung einer Hochstimmung sicher wertvoll und vielleicht oft sogar unentbehrlich; wenn aber nicht ein Mann da ist, der hinter diesem Nebelangriff die praktische Vorbereitung zur Tat trifft und entschlossen ist zu handeln, bleiben sie wirkungslos." (*Memoiren,* p. 80.)

This idea, which has a kernel of truth in it, is partly directed against Hitler: he made speeches, while I, Röhm, tended to business. According to Röhm, the soldier comes before the politician. But it was the politician who ousted the soldier.

February 12

Today *Popu* and *Huma* are in transports of joy because 100,000 "antifascists" marched across the Place de la République. *"Quel admirable peuple!"* writes Blum. These people are always surprised when the masses respond to their call. And they have good reason to be surprised, since for decades now they have done nothing but abuse the confidence of the masses. 100,000! But the *condottieri* of fascism know that this is only a mob which has gathered today and will disperse tomorrow. Vaillant-Couturier, the snob at whose hands Marxist morality was transformed into cynical license, concludes from the demonstration on the Place de la République that the fascist leagues must be disarmed and dissolved right now, *sans délai!*

One can't help recalling, apropos of this, what happened when General Gröner, then Minister of the Interior, issued a ban against Hitler's army, the S.A., in his decree of April 13, 1932. Röhm relates in connection with this: *"Aber nur die Uniformen und Abzeichen waren verschwunden. Nach wie vor übte die S.A. auf dem Truppenübungsplatz Doeberitz sowie auf anderen reichseigen Plätzen. Nur trat sie jetzt nicht mehr als S.A. auf, sondern als Verein Deutscher Volksport."*

One must add that General Gröner was not only Minister of the Interior, but also Minister of the Reichswehr. In his first capacity he "banned" the S.A., out of considerations of parliamentary opportunism, while in the second he provided them, at the government's expense, with all the conveniences they needed in order to continue their development. This highly indicative political incident fully reveals the hopeless stupidity of demands for disarming the fascists.

The banning of the military leagues — supposing the French government should find it necessary to resort to this measure (which, generally speaking, is by no means out of the question) — would only force the fascists to adopt some superficial camouflage of their military preparations, but would in fact make it utterly impossible for the workers legally to prepare to defend themselves. Their central slogan, the "united front," seems made to order as a means of helping the bourgeois reaction drive the proletarian vanguard underground.

* * *

On the subject of the Proudhonist-Anarchist Congress in 1874 Engels wrote contemptuously to Sorge: *"Allgemeine Uneinigkeit über alles Wesentliche verdeckt dadurch dass man nicht debattiert, sondern nur erzählt und anhört."* A remarkably apt formula, which fits the deliberations of the London-Amsterdam bloc to perfection. But nowadays "associations" of this kind have immeasurably less vitality than they had sixty years ago!

* * *

The change in the tone of *Le Temps* is most remarkable. Hardly anything remains of its former Olympian condemnation of the dictatorships of both right and left. Now its editorials eulogize Mussolinism as a means of salvation "if worse comes to worst." Its feature articles provide advertisement for the *Jeunesses Patriotes* and the like. Notre-Dame won't help Flandin.

Chubar's transfer from Kharkov to Moscow somehow passed unnoticed when it happened, and even now I find it hard to recollect just when it did take place. But this move has a political meaning: Chubar is a "substitute" in the sense that sooner or later he is going to crowd Molotov out altogether. Rudzutak and Mezhlauk, the two other substitutes, are not fit for the job: the former has gone to seed and gotten lazy, while the latter is politically too insignificant. In any event, Molotov is living under guard with an escort of potential successors and spends his time meditating on his mortal hour.

* * *

There is no creature more disgusting than a petty bourgeois engaged in primary accumulation. I have never had the opportunity to observe this type as closely as I do now.

February 13

The "leaders" of the proletariat continue to vie with each other in demonstrating to the Reaction their cowardice, their rottenness, their truly doglike readiness to lick the hand that holds the whip over them. And the first prize, of course, goes to Blum. How magnificently the people of Paris behaved on the 10th! How calm they were! How disciplined! The government should have understood *"de quel côté était la volonté populaire."* Flandin was berated in Notre-Dame, while we did not utter a word that might have offended Régnier. And so on. In a word: "There is nothing for you to fear from our side. How then can you refuse to disarm the fascists for us?" But when did the bourgeoisie ever concede anything to those it did not fear?

* * *

Engels is undoubtedly one of the finest, best integrated and noblest personalities in the gallery of great men. To recreate his image would be a gratifying task. It is also a historical duty. On Prinkipo I worked on a book about Marx and Engels, but the preliminary materials were burned in a fire. I doubt that I will be able to return to this subject again. It would be good to finish the book on Lenin so as to move on to more timely work, a book on capitalism in the stage of disintegration.

Christianity created the figure of Christ to humanize the elusive Lord of Hosts and bring him nearer to mortal men. Alongside the Olympian Marx, Engels is more "human," more approachable. How well they complement one another! Or rather, how consciously Engels endeavors to complement Marx; all his life he uses himself up in this task. He regards it as his mission and finds in it his gratification. And this without a shadow of self-sacrifice — always himself, always full of life, always superior to his environment and his age, with immense intellectual interests, with a true fire of genius always blazing in the forge of thought. Against the background of their everyday lives, Engels gains tremendously in stature by comparison with Marx — though of course Marx's stature is not in the least diminished by this. I remember that after reading the Marx-Engels correspondence on my military train, I spoke to Lenin of my admiration for the figure of Engels. My point was just this, that when viewed in his relationship with the titan Marx, faithful Fred gains — rather than diminishes — in stature. Lenin expressed his approval of this idea with alacrity, even with delight. He loved Engels very deeply, and particularly for his wholeness of character and all-round humanity. I remember how we examined with some excitement a portrait of Engels as a young man, discovering in it the traits which became so prominent in his later life.

When you have had enough of the prose of the Blums, the Cachins, and the Thorezes, when you have swallowed your fill of the microbes of pettiness and insolence, obsequiousness and ignorance, there is no better way of clearing your lungs than by reading the correspondence of Marx and Engels, both to each other and to other people. In their epigrammatic allusions and characterizations, sometimes paradoxical, but always well thought out and to the point, there is so much instruction, so much mental freshness and mountain air! They always lived on the heights.

February 14

Engels' prognoses are always optimistic. Not infrequently they run ahead of the actual course of events. But is it possible in general to make historical predictions which — to use a French expression [*brûler les étapes*] — would not burn [skip] some of the intermediate stages?

In the last analysis E. is always right. What he says in his letters to Mme. Wischnewetsky about the development of England and the United States was fully confirmed only in the postwar epoch, forty or fifty years later. But it certainly was confirmed! Who among the great bourgeois statesmen had even an inkling of the present situation of the Anglo-Saxon powers? The Lloyd Georges, the Baldwins, the Roosevelts, not to mention the MacDonalds, seem even today (in fact, today even more than yesterday) like blind puppies alongside the farsighted old Engels. And how thickheaded all these Keyneses are to proclaim that the Marxist prognoses have been refuted!

* * *

Insofar as I can judge by the newspapers sent to me, Stalin's lackeys in France — Thorez & Co. — have formed a veritable plot with the right Social Democratic leaders for a campaign against the "Trotskyists," beginning with the youth organizations. How much time did Stalin and Bukharin spend calling us the "Social Democratic deviation," and then "Social Fascists"? Despite all the difference in the historical situation, the bloc of Blum and Cachin and their common front against "Trotskyism" is amazingly similar to the bloc of Kerensky and Tseretelli in 1917 and their persecution of Bolshevism. The points of similarity lie in the shallowness of the "radical" petty bourgeois, his panic in the face of any menacing situation, his consternation when he feels the ground slipping from under him, and his hatred for those who say openly what he is and what is going to happen to him.

The difference between them — and, alas, a considerable difference it is — lies in the fact that (a) conservative workers' organizations like the S.F.I.O. and the C.G.T. are immeasurably more important in France than they were in Russia in 1917; (b) Bolshevism has been compromised by Stalin's shameful caricature of a party; (c) the entire authority of the Soviet State has been marshaled to disorganize and demoralize the proletarian vanguard. The historic battle in France has not yet been lost. But fascism has invaluable helpers in Blum and the lackeys of Stalin. Thorez has turned inside out all the reasoning, all the arguments and methods of Thälmann. But the politics of Stalinism remain essentially the same, even turned inside out. In Germany the two party organizations of the Social Democrats and the Communists diverted the attention of the workers from the approaching danger by their ostentatious, distorted, unbalanced, fraudulent way of fighting it; in France the same organizations have reached an agreement as to what illusions will best distract the workers' attention from reality. The result is the same!

* * *

The honest, incorruptible, nationalist *Temps* is exposing *"les machines politiques qui ne sont souvent que le nuage artificiel derrière lequel se dissimulent les intérêts particuliers."* It is a mixture of Quaker and Tartuffe, but both the Quaker and Tartuffe have been modernized to suit the epoch of Oustric and Stavisky. The organ of the *Comité des Forges* is exposing *"les intérêts particuliers"!* The *Comité des Forges* is making the whole French press serve its interests. Not a single Radical paper dares to publish anything, for instance, on the fascist-clerical terror which reigns in the hospitals of the *Comité des Forges* against revolutionary workers: if their political allegiance is discovered, they are thrown out of the hospital just before they are to be operated on. The editor of a democratic newspaper, a Radical Socialist, Freemason and the like, replies: "I can't publish anything. Last year, for an article against someone in the *Comité des F.*, my paper, through Havas, was deprived of 20,000 francs' worth of advertisements." How then could the official paper of de Wendel do otherwise than expose the "special interests" in the name of the national good?

In 1925 (or 1924?) Krassin, then Soviet political representative in France, conducted negotiations with the director of *Le Temps*. He reported on them at a session of the Politburo so that he might obtain the necessary directives. The proposals of *Le Temps* were as follows: (a) the editors would within a given time send a correspondent to Moscow who would begin by writing reports that were critical, but dispassionate in tone; (b) the campaign against the U.S.S.R. in the editorial columns would be stopped; (c) a few months later — six, as I remember — the paper would begin to adopt a line favorable to the U.S.S.R. in foreign affairs; (d) the reports from Moscow would become favorable; (e) in their second editorial column (on domestic politics) the editors would be left completely free to criticize Bolshevism; (f) the Soviet government would pay *Le Temps* a million francs a year. Krassin made an initial bid of a half million and went up to 750,000, at which point the negotiations were interrupted. Krassin was now asking the Politburo whether he should go any further. The question was decided in the negative, not only for the sake of economy in the expenditure of foreign currency, but also for diplomatic reasons: there was no hope for agreement with France at that time, and it was deemed wiser to postpone the operation.

If anyone will take the trouble to look through *Le Temps* for 1933 and 1934, he will see that the deal had by then been consummated completely, after a delay of nine years! *

No one would blame the Soviet government for trying to buy the bourgeois press and trying to do so without being

* As I have said, it is difficult for me to decide whether to assign these negotiations to 1924 or 1925, although in Moscow I could determine the date without any trouble. In 1924 the director of *Le Temps* was Emile Hébrard, the associate of the tsarist agent Rafalovich. In 1925 Emile was replaced by old Adrien: such was the modest tribute which vice unmasked paid to virtue. I suppose that no matter what the date, Krassin conducted his negotiations with Emile, but I cannot be certain, since at that time I was not interested in the personalities involved in the affair. In fact, they are of no importance even now. *Le Temps* is *Le Temps*. The generations succeed one another; venality remains.

overcharged. The baseness lies in the attempt of Stalin's clique to make the bourgeois press a weapon in the fight against their own party.

[*Enclosure*]

It has long been known that the "Trotskyists" constitute the "advance guard of the counterrevolutionary bourgeoisie." This fact was demonstrated not so much by the Latvian consul as by the other European and American consuls who have refused me visas. However, there is no need to go beyond the Kirov affair to determine how the sympathies of the bourgeoisie are disposed — or their interests, which indeed is almost the same thing.

Stalin's calumny of Zinoviev and Kamenev, despite its obvious mendacity, was reproduced without criticism by the entire French press. My own brief factual announcement to the effect that I was not acquainted with the "consul" was not printed in a single bourgeois newspaper in France. The account in *Le Temps* is especially instructive. The Moscow correspondent of that paper several times comforted its readers with the assurance that all the groups now being crushed by Stalin stand to the *left* of him, and that consequently there was no cause for alarm. The same correspondent *three times* (!) telegraphed that the consul had *agreed* to transmit letters to Trotsky, whereas in fact the consul had *begged* for such a letter. My dry factual correction was not printed by the editors of *Le Temps*. The same correspondent has transformed Evdokimov into a "Trotskyist," and in one of his recent telegrams speaks of the "troika" [triumvirate] of Trotsky, Zinoviev and Kamenev in order to make his readers forget about the "troika" of Stalin, Zinoviev and Kamenev. And so on, endlessly. The resourceful journalist and his paper know what they are doing. In the last analysis *Le Temps* is performing the same function in this area as *L'Humanité,* only more carefully, cleverly, and subtly. It is not easy to judge which of them is more disinterested. All the same, I think *L'Humanité* costs them less.

[*End of enclosure.*]

On October 10, 1888, Engels wrote to New York:

"In Frankreich blamieren sich die Radikalen an der Regierung mehr als zu hoffen war. Gegenüber den Arbeitern verleugnen sie ihr ganzes eigenes altes Programm und treten als reine Opportunisten auf, holen den Opportunisten die Kastanien aus dem Feuer, waschen ihnen die schmutzige Wäsche. Das wäre ganz vortrefflich, wäre nicht Boulanger und jagten sie noch diesem die Massen fast zwangsmässig in die Arme." (306)

These lines seem to have been written for our own time. In 1934 the Radicals proved just as incapable of ruling France as they were in 1888. Just as before, they are only good for pulling the reaction's chestnuts out of the fire. All this would be splendid if there were a revolutionary party in existence. But there is none. Or, still worse, there is a revolting caricature of such a party. And the Radicals are driving the masses in the direction of fascism, just as a half-century ago they drove them toward Boulangism.

Under these conditions the Stalinists form a bloc with the Radicals "against fascism" and try to force the Socialists to join them — a windfall the latter never even dared to dream of. Like half-trained monkeys, some Stalinists even now keep on grumbling about the bloc: what we need is not parliamentary deals with the Radicals, but a "people's front" against fascism! One feels as if one were reading an official paper from the madhouse at Charenton! A parliamentary bloc with the Radicals, no matter how criminal from the point of view of the interests of socialism, makes — or at least made — political sense as a device in the electoral and parliamentary strategy of democratic reformers. But what possible sense could there be in an extraparliamentary bloc with a purely parliamentary party which by its very social composition is incapable of any extraparliamentary mass action whatsoever? The bourgeois elite of the party is scared to death of its own mass base. To accept once every four years the votes of the peasants, petty tradesmen and officials — to this Herriot magnanimously agrees. But to lead them into an open struggle means to conjure up spirits of which he is much more afraid than he is of fascism. The so-called "popular front," i.e., the bloc with the Radicals for extraparliamentary action, is the most criminal mockery of the people that the working-class parties have permitted themselves since the war — and they have permitted themselves a great deal. While Herriot holds the stirrup for Flandin and the Radical Minister of the Interior trains the police to suppress the workers, the Stalinists make up the Radicals to look like leaders of the people, promising to collaborate with them in crushing fascism, which itself derives its chief political nourishment from the falsity and lies of radicalism. Is it not a madhouse?

If the inevitable reckoning for these crimes — and what a terrible reckoning it will be! — fell only on the clique of Stalinist lackeys, hired adventurers, and bureaucratic cynics, one could only say, "Serves them right!" The misfortune is that it is the workers who will have to pay the score.

There is something particularly nightmarish in the fact that the oppressed masses searching for a way out are being offered, under the labels of Marxism and Bolshevism, the very ideas in the fight against which Marxism was shaped and Bolshevism developed. Truly, *Vernunft wird Unsinn, Wohltat — Plage!*

* * *

All the *serious* bourgeois press supports, covers up for, and defends the armed leagues. It has finally penetrated the bourgeois consciousness that these leagues are a necessity and a source of salvation. The economic difficulties are too great. Revolutionary outbursts are possible, even inevitable. The police are not enough. To call out the troops, especially in view of the one-year training period, is too risky: the troops might waver. What could be more reliable than hand-picked and trained fascist detachments? They will not waver, and they will not allow the army to waver. Is it surprising then that the bourgeoisie clings to its armed leagues with both hands?

And Blum asks the bourgeois government for a small favor — that it *disarm itself*. No more than that. Day after day the Paul Faures, the Vaillant-Couturiers, the Zyromskys repeat this stupid and shameful "demand," which can only increase the fascists' confidence in their future. Not one of these musical-comedy heroes understands the seriousness of the situation. They are doomed.

One o'clock in the morning. It is a long time since I have written at such a late hour. I have already tried several times to go to bed, but indignation gets me up again every time.

During the cholera epidemic the ignorant, frightened, and embittered Russian peasants killed their doctors, destroyed medicines, and tore down the quarantine huts. The hounding of the "Trotskyists," the banishments, expulsions, and denunciations — with the support of a part of the workers — do they not remind one of the senseless convulsions of the desperate peasants? The "leaders" of the working-class parties act as instigators. Small detachments serve as strong-arm squads. Distractedly the masses watch the brutal beating of the doctors, the only people who know both the disease and its cure.

February 15

Le Temps has published a very sympathetic report from its Moscow correspondent about the new privileges granted to the *kolkhozniks* [collective farmers], especially in regard to their acquiring ownership of horses, cattle, and other livestock. Certain further concessions to the petty bourgeois tendencies of the peasant seem to be in preparation. At this stage it is hard to predict the point at which they will manage to hold the line against the present retreat. But the retreat itself, brought on as it was by the extremely crude bureaucratic illusions of the preceding period, was not difficult to foresee. Since the fall of 1929 the *Bulletin* of the Russian Opposition has been sounding the alarm against irresponsible methods of collectivization. "In this manipulation of uncoordinated tempos the foundation is being laid for an inevitable crisis in the immediate future." The rest is well known: the slaughter of the cattle, the famine of 1933, the untold number of victims, and the series of political crises. At the present time the retreat is proceeding at full speed. For this very reason Stalin is once again forced to cut down everyone and everything that stands to the left of him.

Revolution by its very nature is sometimes compelled to take in more territory than it is capable of holding. Retreats are possible — when there is territory to retreat from. But this general law by no means justifies wholesale collectivization. Its absurdities were not the result of elemental pressure from the masses, but of bureaucratic bungling. Instead of regulating the collectivization according to the productive and technical resources of the country and instead of extending the radius of collectivization in breadth and depth according to the dictates of experience, the frightened bureaucrats began to drive the frightened muzhiks into the collective farms with the knout. Stalin's narrow empiricism and utter lack of vision are nowhere more starkly revealed than in his commentaries on the subject of wholesale collectivization. But now, the retreat is being carried out without commentaries.

Le Temps, *February 16:*

"Nos parlementaires prononcent volontiers l'oraison funèbre du libéralisme économique. Comment ne sentent-ils pas qu'ils préparent ainsi la leur, et que si la liberté économique mourait le Parlement la suivrait dans la tombe?" [*Clipping pasted in and underlined in pencil; quotation marks added in ink.*]

Remarkable words! Without suspecting it, the "idealists" of *Le Temps* subscribe to one of the most important premises of Marxism: that parliamentary democracy is merely a superstructure built over the system of bourgeois competition, with which it stands and falls. But this involuntary borrowing from Marxism makes the political position of *Le Temps* immeasurably stronger than that of the Socialists and Radical Socialists, who want to preserve democracy while giving it a "different" economic content. These phrase-mongers cannot understand that the economy and political regime of a country are related like muscles and skin, not like canned food and the can.

Conclusion: parliamentary democracy is as much doomed as free competition. The only question is, who will be their heir?

February 17

I imagine an old doctor, devoid of neither education nor experience, who day after day has to watch quacks and charlatans doctor to death a person dear to him, knowing that this person could be certainly cured if only the elementary rules of medicine were observed. That would approximately be the way I feel as I watch the criminal work of the "leaders" of the French proletariat. Conceit? No, a deep and indestructible conviction.

Our life here differs very little from imprisonment. We are shut up in our house and yard and meet people no more often than we would at visiting hours in a prison. True, within the last few months we have acquired a radio, but such things probably exist even in certain prisons, at least in America (not in France, of course). We listen almost exclusively to concerts, which now occupy a rather prominent place in our daily routine. For the most part, I listen to music superficially, while working. Sometimes music helps me to write, sometimes it hinders; in general I would say that it helps me to make first drafts of my ideas, but hinders me from working them up. N., as always, listens with absorption and concentration. Right now we are listening to Rimsky-Korsakov.

The radio reminds one how broad and varied life is and at the same time gives an extremely economical and compact expression to this variety. In short, it is an instrument perfectly suited to a prison.

February 18

In 1926, when Zinoviev and Kamenev joined the Opposition after more than three years of plotting with Stalin against me, they gave me a number of not unnecessary warnings:

"Do you think that Stalin is now considering how to reply to your arguments?" This was approximately what Kamenev said, in reference to my criticism of the Stalin-Bukharin-Molotov policies in China, England, etc. "You are mistaken. He is thinking of how to destroy you."

"?"

"Morally, and if possible, physically as well. To slander you, to trump up a military conspiracy, and then, when the ground has been prepared, to perpetrate a terroristic act. Stalin is conducting the war on a different plane from you. Your weapons are ineffective against him."

On another occasion the same Kamenev told me, "I know him only too well from the old days when we worked together, from the time we spent together in exile, and from the period of collaboration in the 'troika.' As soon as we broke with Stalin, Zinoviev and I drew up something like a testament, in which we gave warning that in the event of our 'accidental' death, Stalin should be considered responsible. This document is kept in a safe place. I advise you to do the same."

Zinoviev told me, not without embarrassment, "Do you think that Stalin has not discussed the question of your physical removal? He has considered and discussed it thoroughly. He has always been held back by the same thought, that the young people would pin the responsibility on him personally, and would respond by acts of terrorism. He therefore believed that he first had to disperse the ranks of the oppositionist youth. But a job postponed is not a job abandoned. Take the necessary precautions."

Kamenev was undoubtedly right when he said that Stalin — and for that matter also he himself and Zinoviev in the preceding period — was conducting the struggle on a different plane and with different weapons. But the very possibility of such a mode of struggle had been created by the formation and consolidation of a separate and self-sufficient social milieu — the Soviet bureaucracy. Stalin was fighting to concentrate power in the hands of the bureaucracy and to expel the opposition from his ranks, while we were fighting for the interests of the international revolution and thus setting ourselves against the conservatism of the bureaucracy and its longing for tranquility, prosperity and comfort. In view of the prolonged decline in the international revolution the victory of the bureaucracy — and consequently of Stalin — was foreordained. The result which the idle observers and fools attribute to the personal forcefulness of Stalin, or at least to his exceptional cunning, stemmed from causes lying deep in the dynamics of historical forces. Stalin emerged as the half-conscious expression of the second chapter of the revolution, its "morning after."

One day during our sojourn in Alma-Ata (Central Asia) a certain Soviet engineer came to see me, supposedly on his own initiative and supposedly sympathetic toward me personally. He inquired about our living conditions, expressed his regret about them, and in passing very cautiously asked, "Don't you think that some steps toward reconciliation are possible?" Clearly, the engineer had been sent surreptitiously in order to feel my pulse. I answered him to the effect that at that moment there could be no question of reconciliation, not because I *did not want* it, but because Stalin *could not* make his peace with me. He was forced to pursue to the end the course set him by the bureaucracy. "How will it end?" "It will come to a sticky end," I answered. "Stalin cannot settle it any other way." My visitor was visibly startled; he obviously had not expected such an answer, and soon left.

I think that this conversation was an important factor in the decision to deport me abroad. It is possible that Stalin had considered such a course even earlier, but had encountered oppositon in the Politburo. Now he had a strong argument: T. himself had announced that the conflict would come to a bloody end. Exile was the only way out.

The arguments which Stalin used in favor of my exile were published by me at the proper time in the *Bulletin* of the Russian Opposition. See [*reference never filled in*].

But how could it be that Stalin was not restrained by the thought of the Comintern? Undoubtedly he underestimated this danger. In his mind the concept of power is inextricably bound up with the concept of the Party *apparat*. He began to engage in open polemics only when he had assured himself in advance of having the last word. Kamenev was right: he does his fighting on another plane. Precisely because of this he underestimated the danger of a struggle purely on the plane of ideas.

February 20

During 1924–1928 Stalin and his cohorts directed a growing hatred against my secretariat. It seemed to them that my little "*apparat*" was the source of all evil. It took me some time to grasp the reasons for their almost superstitious fear of the little group — five or six people — of my collaborators. These high dignitaries, whose speeches and articles were written by secretaries, seriously imagined that they could render an adversary helpless by depriving him of his "office staff." In due course I told in print the story of the tragic fate of my collaborators: Glazman driven to suicide, Butov dead in a G.P.U. prison, Blumkin shot, Sermuks and Poznansky banished. Stalin did not foresee that even without a secretariat I could carry on systematic literary work which, in its turn, could further the creation of a new "*apparat*." Even the cleverest bureaucrats display an incredible short-sightedness in certain questions!

The years of my new emigration, which have been taken up with literary work and correspondence, have brought forth thousands of conscious and active adherents in different countries and parts of the world. The struggle for the Fourth International is ricocheting back against the Soviet bureaucracy. Hence, after a prolonged interruption, a new campaign against Trotskyism. Stalin would now give a great deal to be able to retract the decision to deport me: how tempting it would be to stage a "show" trial! But the past cannot be brought back. One is obliged to look for other methods than a trial. And of course, Stalin is doing just that

— in the spirit of the warnings by Kamenev and Zinoviev. But the danger of exposure is too great. The distrust which the workers of the West feel toward Stalin's machinations could only have increased since the time of the Kirov affair. Stalin will unquestionably resort to a terroristic act in two cases (most probably with the collaboration of White organizations, in which the G.P.U. has many agents, or with the help of the French fascists, who would not be hard to approach): if there is a threat of war, or if his own position deteriorates gravely. Of course, there could also be a third case, and a fourth . . . It is hard to say how severe a blow a terroristic act of this sort would prove to be for the Fourth International, but in any case it would be fatal for the Third . . .

We shall see. And if we don't, then others will.

* * *

Rakovsky is graciously admitted to the solemn assemblies and receptions for foreign ambassadors and bourgeois journalists. One great revolutionary less, one petty official more!

* * *

Zyromsky wants to form an alliance with Stalin. It is reported that Otto Bauer is planning to go to Moscow. Both facts are easy to explain. All the scared opportunists of the Second International inevitably gravitate these days toward the Soviet bureaucracy. They did not suceed in adapting to the bourgeois state, so they want to try adapting to the workers' state. The essence of their nature is adaptation, yielding to force. They will never make a revolution. We need new people, newly selected, newly trained, newly tempered — in short, a new generation.

March 1935

March 6

It is more than two weeks since I have touched this diary — ill health and pressing work. The last *Conseil national* of the French Socialist Party demonstrates the strength of the pressure brought to bear on the parliamentary leadership. Léon Blum admitted that in Tours, in 1920, he did not quite have an adequate understanding of the problem of the conquest of power, when he believed that the conditions for socialization should be created first, and after that . . . But why fight for power if the "conditions of socialization" can be created without it? Or does B. mean economic and not political conditions? These conditions are not being created but rather destroyed by delaying the struggle for power: capitalism is not developing but beginning to rot. B. does not understand the situation even now, after repudiating his views of the Tours period. According to him, he is driven toward revolutionary struggle not by the general condition of capitalism, but by the threat from the fascists, whom he considers less a product of the decomposition of capitalism than an *external* danger which jeopardizes the peaceful socialization of democracy (an old illusion of Jaurès).

It is understandable that the leaders of the bourgeoisie are blind to the laws of capitalism in decline: a dying man does not want to and cannot recognize the stages of his own dissolution. But the blindness of Blum and Co. . . . it is perhaps the clearest proof that these gentlemen represent not the advance guard of the proletariat but only the left and most frightened flank of the bourgeoisie.

* * *

After the World War B. believed (and essentially does so even now) that conditions were not yet ripe for socialization. What naïve dreamers, then, were Marx and Engels, who in the second half of the nineteenth century expected and prepared for socialist revolution! For Blum there exists (insofar as anything at all in this sphere exists for him) some absolute economic "ripeness" of society for socialism, which can be determined from purely objective indications. I fought against this mechanistic, fatalistic conception as early as 1905 (see *The Results of the Revolution and its Perspectives*). Since then the October Revolution has ocurred, not to mention all the rest; but those parliamentary dilettantes have learned *nothing.*

[*March*] 7

In the minutes of the July-August Joint Plenum of the Central Committee and Central Executive Committee for 1927 (I think precisely in these minutes), one can read — those to whom these secret minutes are available, that is — a special statement by M. Ulyanova in defense of Stalin. The essence of the statement is as follows: (1) shortly before his second stroke Lenin broke off personal relations with Stalin for a purely personal reason; (2) if Lenin had not valued Stalin as a revolutionary he would not have turned to him with a request for the kind of favor that could be expected only from a real revolutionary. There is a conscious omission in the statement which concerns a certain very critical episode. I want to record it here.

First of all, about M. I. Ulyanova, the youngest sister of

The house in Domène, where this *Diary* began.
View from the road.

Side entrance of the house in Domène.

"Will it be for long? Perhaps months . . ."

(February 7)

глупое и постыдное „требование", кото-
рое должно только ~~во~~ укреплять уверенность
фашистов в своем завтрашнем дне. Ни
один из этих ~~вожд~~ ~~вождей~~ опереточных
героев не понимает серьезности положения.
Они обречены.

Час ночи. Давно я не писал в такой
поздний час. ~~Негодование~~ Я пробовал уже
несколько раз ложиться, но негодование
каждый раз снова поднимало меня.

Во время холерных эпидемий темная запу-
ганные и ожесточенные русские крестьяне
убивали ~~иногда~~ врачей, ~~разбивали~~ [уничтожали] лекар-
ства, громили холерные бараки. ~~Подстре-~~
~~кателями выступали самые темные и р~~
Разве травля „троцкистов", изгнания,
[доносы, - принудительно части рабочих -]
исключения, не напоминают ~~эту~~

"Indignation gets me up again every time."

(February 14)

18 февраля.

В 1926 г., когда Зиновьев и Каменев, после трех с лишним лет совместного со Сталиным заговора ~~конспирации~~ против меня ~~со Сталиным~~, присоединились к оппозиции, они ~~очень сдержанно и осторожно~~ сделали мне ряд назидательных ~~предостережений~~ предостережений.

— Вы думаете, Сталин размышляет сейчас над тем, как возразить ~~[illegible]~~ вам? — ~~[illegible]~~ говорил примерно Каменев по поводу моей критики ~~сталинской~~ политики Сталина-Бухарина-Молотова в Китае, в Англии и пр. — Вы ошибаетесь. Он думает о том, как вас уничтожить.

— ?

— Морально, а если возможно, то и физически. Оклеветать, подкинуть военный заговор, а затем, когда почва будет подготовлена, подстроить террористический акт. Сталин ведет войну в другой плоскости, чем вы. Ваше оружие против него недействительно.

“ ‘Stalin is conducting the war on a different plane from you.’ ”

(February 18)

9 апр.

Выборы в Данциге дополнили урок саарского плебисцита. Наци собрали только 60%: хотя не было вопроса о присоединении к Германии. Террор наци в Данциге был больше, чем в Сааре: это показывает, что один террор не решает. Социал-дем. почти сохранили свои голоса (38.000) 1933 г., как и католики (31.000). Коммунисты упали с 14,566 до 8,990! В Сааре нельзя было различить голоса этих партий. Тем важнее данцигский урок! Коммунисты потеряли больше трети, с-д остались на старом уровне. Когда надвигается революция, больше всего выигрывает крайняя партия. Вне разгула революции крайняя партия наиболее теряет. В данных условиях данцигские выборы подтверждают прогрессивный паралич Коминтерна.

Dantzig, 8 avril. — Voici les résultats officiels provisoires des élections :

La diminution des suffrages communistes s'explique avant tout par le fait que c'est contre le P.C. qu'a été dirigée essentiellement la terreur nazie et que notre Parti a été réduit pratiquement à l'illégalité.

Les nationaux-socialistes ont obtenu 139.043 suffrages, contre 109.729 le 28 mai 1933.

Les sociaux-démocrates : 38.015 contre 37.882.

Les communistes : 7.990, contre 14.566.

Le centre catholique : 31.525, contre 31.336.

Les nationaux allemands : 9.691 contre 13.596.

Les Polonais : 8.310, contre 6.743.

Les anciens combattants oppositionnels : 382.

Sur 250.498 électeurs inscrits, dont 13.000 venus de l'étranger, on compte 234.956 suffrages valables, soit une proportion d'environ 95 %, contre 92 % en 1933.

La liste nationale-socialiste a donc réuni moins de 60 % des suffrages et n'a pas atteint son objectif des deux tiers qui lui seraient nécessaires pour modifier la Constitution dantzikoise.

L'AVANCE COMMUNISTE

9/IV

	Communistes	S.F.I.O.
1928	8.591	9.385
1932	4.647	6.865
1934	5.218	5.571
1935	6.240	5.462

dans le canton de Carvin

L'Huma 9/IV

En trois mois la C.G.T.U. a recruté 10.000 adhérents nouveaux

Очень важные данные !!!

Un candidat de Flandin battu par un agrarien dans l'Yonne

Dans le canton de Vézelay (Yonne), le candidat agraire, Mary-Gallot, a été élu dimanche conseiller d'arrondissement par 690 voix contre 648 au candidat de l'Alliance démocratique, Cestac, patronné par Flandin.

Le président du conseil est conseiller général de ce même canton et le résultat d'avant-hier ne lui est donc pas précisément favorable.

L'Huma 9/IV → Selon L'Huma Gallot représente le front commun

"Very important data! ! !"

(April 9)

Lenin "Maniasha," as she was called in the family. An old maid, reserved and stubborn, she concentrated all the strength of her unspent love on her brother Vladimir. In his lifetime she remained completely in the background; nobody spoke about her. In taking care of V. I. she vied with N. K. Krupskaya. After his death she emerged into the limelight, or rather she was forced to do so. Through the editorial offices of *Pravda* — she was the secretary of the newspaper — Ulyanova was closely connected with Bukharin. She fell under his influence and in his wake was drawn into the struggle against the Opposition. Ulyanova's jealousy was stengthened by her narrowness and fanaticism, and also by her rivalry with Krupskaya, who consistently and firmly refused to act against her conscience. During this period Ulyanova began to make speeches at party meetings, write reminiscences, etc., and it must be said that not one of Lenin's intimates revealed such lack of understanding as this sister who was so unreservedly devoted to him. At the beginning of 1926 Krupskaya — albeit not for long — joined the Opposition, through the Zinoviev-Kamenev group. At that precise moment, the Stalin-Bukharin faction was trying every means of elevating M. Ulyanova's standing and significance to counterbalance Krupskaya.

I have told in my autobiography how Stalin tried to isolate Lenin during the second period of his illness, before his second stroke. He was calculating that Lenin would never recover, and was trying with all his might to prevent Lenin from communicating his views in writing. (Thus he attempted to prevent the publication of Lenin's article on the organization of a Central Control Commission to fight against bureaucratism, i.e., chiefly against Stalin's faction.) Krupskaya served as the main source of information for the sick Lenin. Stalin began to persecute Krupskaya, and in the rudest way. It was for this very reason that the conflict took place. At the beginning of March (I think on the 5th), 1923, Lenin wrote — dictated — a letter to Stalin breaking off all personal and comradely relations with him. Thus the basis of the conflict was not at all personal, and with Lenin it could not have been personal . . .

What request of Lenin's, then, did Ulyanova have in mind in her written statement? When Lenin felt worse again, in February or the very first days of March, he summoned Stalin and addressed to him an insistent request to bring him some poison. Afraid lest he lose the power of speech again and become a toy in the hands of the doctors, Lenin wanted to remain the master of his fate. It was no accident that at one time he had expressed his approval of Lafargue, who preferred by his own act to *"join the majority"* [in English] rather than to live an invalid.

M. Ulyanova wrote, "Such a request could be directed only to a revolutionary . . ." It is beyond dispute that Lenin considered Stalin a staunch revolutionary. But this fact alone was not enough to make Lenin apply to him with such an exceptional request. Obviously Lenin must have thought that Stalin was the only one of the leading revolutionists who would not refuse to give him poison. It should not be forgotten that this request was made a few days before the final rupture. Lenin knew Stalin, his schemes and plans, his treatment of Krupskaya. He knew that all Stalin's actions were based on the assumption that he would not recover. Under these conditions Lenin applied to Stalin for poison. It is possible that this gesture — besides its main purpose — was designed to test both Stalin and the forced optimism of the doctors. Anyhow, Stalin did not comply with the request, but reported it to the Politburo. Everybody protested;

the doctors still maintained there were grounds for hope; Stalin kept his own counsel . . .

In 1926 Krupskaya reported to me a remark Lenin had made about Stalin: "He lacks the most elementary human honesty." Essentially the same idea is expressed in the "Testament," only more cautiously. The tendency which at that time was still in its initial stage has only now reached its full development. Lies, falsification, forgery, and judicial perversion have assumed a scale hitherto unheard of in history, and, as the Kirov affair demonstrates, constitute a direct threat to the Stalinist regime.

March 9

Aleksey Tolstoy's novel, *Peter I,* is a work remarkable for the immediacy of its feeling for the remote Russian past. Of course this is not "proletarian literature": as a writer A. Tolstoy has his roots in old Russian literature — and world literature as well, naturally. But undoubtedly it was the Revolution — by the law of contrast — that gave him (and not him alone) an especially keen feeling for the peculiar nature of Russian antiquity — immobile, wild and unwashed. It taught him something more: to look beneath the ideological conceptions, fantasies and superstitions for the simple vital interests of the various social groups and of the individuals belonging to them. With great artistic penetration A. Tolstoy lays bare the hidden material underpinnings of the ideological conflicts in Peter's Russia. In this way individual psychological realism is elevated to social realism. This is undoubtedly an achievement of the Revolution as an immediate experience and of Marxism as a general doctrine.

Mauriac, a French novelist whom I do not know, an

Academician (which is a poor recommendation), wrote or said recently: we shall recognize the U.S.S.R. when it produces a new novel of the calibre of Tolstoy or Dostoevsky. Mauriac was apparently making a distinction between this artistic, idealistic criterion and a Marxist, materialistic one, based on relations of production. Actually, there is no contradiction here. In the preface to my book *Literature and Revolution* I wrote about twelve years ago:

"But even a successful solution of the elementary problems of food, clothing, shelter, and even of literacy, would in no way signify a complete victory of the new historic principle, that is, of Socialism. Only a movement of scientific thought on a national scale and the development of a new art would signify that the historic seed has not only grown into a plant, but has even flowered. In this sense, the development of Art is the highest test of the vitality and significance of each epoch."

However, it is impossible in any sense to represent the novel of A. Tolstoy as a "flower" of the new epoch. It has already been stated why this is true. And the novels which are officially regarded as "proletarian art" (in a period of complete liquidation of classes!) are as yet totally lacking in artistic significance. Of course, there is nothing "alarming" in this. It takes some time for a complete overturn of social foundations, customs and assumptions to produce an artistic crystallization along new axes. How much time? One cannot say offhand, but a long time. Art is always carried in the baggage train of a new epoch, and great art — the novel — is an especially heavy load. That there has been no great new art so far is quite natural and, as I have said, should not and cannot alarm anyone. What can be alarming, though, are the revolting imitations of a new art written on the order of the bureaucracy. The incongruities, falsity and ignorance of the present "Soviet" Bonapartism attempting to establish unlimited control over art — these things make impossible any artistic creativity whatsoever, the first condition for which is *sincerity*. An old engineer can perhaps build a turbine reluctantly; it would not be first-rate, precisely because it had been built reluctantly, but it would serve its purpose. But one cannot, however, write a poem *reluctantly*.

It is not by accident that Aleksey Tolstoy retreated to the end of the seventeenth century and the beginning of the eighteenth in order to gain the freedom essential to the artist.

March 10

I have looked carefully through the documents of the economic "plan" of the C.G.T. What poverty of thought covered up with ridiculous bureaucratic pomposity! And what degrading cowardice toward the employers! These reformers address themselves not to the workers with the aim of arousing them to carry out the plan, but to the employers with the aim of convincing them that the plan is essentially conservative.

Actually, there is no "plan" whatsoever, for an economic plan, in any serious sense of the term, presupposes not algebraic formulas, but definite arithmetical quantities. This, of course, is quite out of the question: in order to form *such* a plan one must be the employer, i.e., one must hold in one's hands all the basic elements of the economy; and this is possible only for the victorious proletariat when it has created its own state.

But even the emptiness and ambiguousness of the algebraic formulas of Jouhaux & Co. would be truly startling if one did not know in advance that those gentlemen are concerned with only one thing: how to distract the attention of the workers from the bankruptcy of trade union reformism.

March 18

It will soon be a year since we were subjected to attack by the authorities at Barbizon. This was the most comic mix-up one could possibly imagine. The operation was directed by *Monsieur le procureur de la République* from Melun, a high personage in the world of jurisprudence. He was accompanied by a little examining magistrate, a *greffier*, who wrote in longhand, a commissary of the *Sûreté générale*, detectives, gendarmes, policemen — numbering in all several dozen. Honest Benno, the "*molosse*," was tearing at his chain; Stella seconded him from behind the house.

The prosecutor announced to me that all this army had come on account of . . . a stolen motorcycle. It was all quite transparent. Rudolf, my German collaborator, had brought the mail on his motorcycle. His headlight had gone out on the way. The gendarmes, who for a long time had been looking for an excuse to penetrate our mysterious cottage, seized upon this incident.

March 21

It's spring, the sun is hot, the violets have been in bloom for about ten days, the peasants are puttering around in the vineyards. Last night we listened to *Die Walküre* from

Bordeaux until midnight. Military service extended to two years. Rearmament of Germany. Preparations for a new "final" war. The peasants peacefully prune their vines and fertilize the furrows between them. Everything is in order.

The Socialists and the Communists write articles against the two-year term, and for the sake of greater impressiveness trot out their largest type. Deep in their hearts the "leaders" hope things will work out somehow. Here also everything is in order.

And yet this order has hopelessly undermined itself. It will collapse with a stench . . .

* * *

Jules Romains is apparently very much concerned about it, since he offers himself as a savior (Society of the Ninth of July). In one of the later books in his epic Romains seems to depict himself under the name of the writer Strigelius (I think that's the right name). This S. has the same aptitude and ability as other writers, but he has something else on top of that. His ability is not only that of a writer. He has discovered that his "ability" (genius) is universal. His capacity is greater than other people's in other fields too, in politics in particular. Hence the Society of the Ninth of July and J. R.'s book on the relations between France and Germany.

No doubt this talented writer has lost his balance a bit. He understands a good deal about politics, but rather visually, i.e., superficially. The deep social springs behind events remain hidden from him. In the sphere of individual psychology he is remarkable, but again not profound. As a writer (and even more as a politician) he is evidently lacking in *character*. He is a spectator, and not a participant.

But only a participant can be a profound spectator. Zola was a participant. That is why, with all his vulgarities and lapses, he is far above Romains: deeper, warmer, more human. J. Romains refers to himself (this time without a pseudonym, by his own name) as *distant* [in French]. This is true. But his *distance* [in French] is not only optical but also moral. His moral lights allow him to see everything only from a certain fixed distance. That is why he seems to be too far away from little Bastide and too close to the murderer Quinette. With a participant, his "*distance*" changes depending on the nature of his participation, while with a spectator it does not. A spectator like Romains can be a *remarkable* writer, but he cannot be a *great* writer.

* * *

I did not finish writing about our last year's "catastrophe" in Barbizon. The "story" was sufficiently spread over the newspapers. What a furious torrent of the stupidest fabrications and unfeigned hatred!

How fine the "*procureur de la République*" was! One should never look at those high dignitaries too closely. He called on me allegedly on account of the stolen motorcycle (our own motorcycle, which Rudolf had been using), but asked immediately what my *real* name was. My passport is in the name of Sedov, my wife's name, which is quite permissible according to Soviet law; but then the *procureur* from Melun is not obliged to know Soviet law. "But you were supposed to settle in Corsica, weren't you?" "And what does that have to do with the stolen motorcycle?" "*Non, non, je parle d'homme à homme.*" But then this was said by way of retreat when it turned out that my passport was stamped with a visa by the *Sûreté générale*. They held

Rudolf for 36 hours, put *menottes* on him, abused him (*sale boche*), beat him — or rather pushed him around. When they finally took him in to me, I moved up a chair for him — he looked distraught; but the *procureur* screamed, "*Non, debout!*" Rudolf sat down without even noticing this screaming. Of all these visitors only the old *greffier* left a favorable impression. And the rest . . .

However, all this does not deserve such a detailed description.

March 22

In Norway the Labor Party has been in power for several days. This will cause little change in the course of European history. But in the course of my life . . . In any case, the question of a *visa* arises. We only passed through Norway on the way from New York to Petersburg in 1917, and I have not retained any memories of the country. I remember Ibsen better: in my youth I wrote about him.

March 23

In his novel *The Rape of Europe* — a "literary" novel, not profound and often pretentious — Fedin demonstrates one thing: the revolution has taught (or forced) Russian writers to pay closer attention to facts which reveal the social dependence of one person upon another. The normal bourgeois novel has two floors: emotions are experienced only in the *bel-étage* (Proust!), while the people in the basement polish shoes and take out chamber-pots. This is rarely mentioned in the novel itself, but presupposed as something quite natural. The hero sighs, the heroine breathes; it follows that they perform other bodily functions too; somebody, then, has to clean up after them. I remember reading a novel of Louÿs called *Amour and Psyche* — an unusually sham and banal concoction, completed, if I am not mistaken, by the unbearable Claude Farrère. Louÿs puts the servants somewhere in the nether regions, so that his enamored hero and heroine never see them. An ideal social system for amorous idlers and their artists!

Essentially Fedin too is primarily interested in the people of the *bel-étage* (in Holland), but he tries, at least in passing, to observe the psychology of the relationship between a chauffeur and a financial magnate and between a sailor and a shipowner. He offers no revelations, but nevertheless he does light up certain corners of those human relationships on which contemporary society rests. The influence of the October Revolution upon literature is still completely a thing of the future!

The radio is playing the *Symphonie héroïque,* Concert Pasdeloup. I envy N[atasha] when she is listening to great music: she listens with all the pores of her soul and body. N. is not a musician, but she is something more than that: her whole nature is musical; in her sufferings as well as in her — infrequent — joys, there is always a deep melody which ennobles all her experiences. Even though she is interested in the small daily facts of politics, she does not usually combine them into one coherent picture. Yet when politics go deep down and demand a complete reaction, N. always finds in her inner music the right note. The same is true of her judgments of people, and not only personal, psychological ones, but also those she makes as a revolutionary. Philistinism, vulgarity, and cowardice can never be concealed from her, even though she is exceptionally lenient toward all minor human vices.

Sensitive people, even quite "simple" people — and children too — instinctively feel the musicality and depth of her nature. Of those who pass her by with indifference or condescension, without noticing the forces concealed in her, one can almost always say with certainty that they are superficial and trivial.

. . . The end of the *Symphonie héroïque.* (It was played in excerpts.)

March 25

Only after the entry of March 23 (about N.) I realized that in the preceding pages I had been keeping a political and literary diary rather than a personal one. And could it actually be otherwise? For politics and literature constitute in essence the content of my personal life. I need only take pen in hand and my thoughts of their own accord arrange themselves for *public* exposition . . . You can't alter this, especially at 55 years of age.

By the way, Lenin (repeating Turgenev) once asked Krzhizhanovsky: "Do you know what is the greatest vice?" Krzhizhanovsky did not know. "To be more than 55 years old." Lenin himself did not live long enough to develop this "vice."

* * *

The results of the election in Blois (Loir-et-Cher), in a district previously held by the Radical, C. Chautemps, were 6,760 votes for the leader of the *Front Paysan,* Dorgères, and 4,848 votes for the Radical. There will be a run-off election. In May, 1932, Chautemps had 11,204 votes and was elected on the first ballot. These are remarkably symptomatic figures. After February 6, 1934, I said that it was the beginning of the collapse of French radicalism and, with it, of the Third Republic. The peasants are abandoning the democratic windbags and humbugs. In France a big fascist party along the lines of the Nazis is not to be expected. It will be sufficient for the Dorgères to undermine "democracy" in various places — and people will be found in Paris to knock it down.

The municipal elections will make evident the undoubted decline of radicalism. Part of the voters will move to the right and part to the left, to the Socialists. These last will lose somewhat to the Communists. Whether the Socialists come out better or worse in the scale than they are now it is hard to predict, but in any case the change will be hardly very significant. The Radicals are bound to lose a *great deal.* The Communists will undoubtedly gain. The reactionary peasant demagogues will also gain. But the municipal election figures reflect only in an extremely weakened form the deeper and more dynamic process of the abandonment of democracy by the petty-bourgeois masses. An audacious military move by the fascists may reveal how far this process has gone — much farther, in any case, than it seems to parliamentary stick-in-the-muds.

The "leaders" of the labor parties and the unions see nothing, understand nothing, are capable of nothing. What a miserable, ignorant, cowardly fraternity they are!

* * *

On June 15, 1885, Engels wrote to old Becker:

"Du hast ganz recht, in Frankreich schleift sich der

Radikalismus kolossal rasch ab. Es ist eigentlich nur noch einer zu verschleissen und das ist Clemenceau. Wenn der drankommit, wird er einen ganzen Haufen Illusionen verlieren, vor allem die, man könne heutzutage eine bürgerliche Republik in Frankreich regieren, ohne zu stehlen und stehlen zu lassen."

And the virtuous *Temps* still keeps on shuddering over the unexpectedness of each new financial scandal!

For a long time Marx and Engels expected that Clemenceau would not remain satisfied with the program of radicalism. They thought him too critical and decisive for this and believed he would become a socialist. Clemenceau, indeed, did not long hold to the position of radicalism (which was created for people like Herriot); but he left it not for socialism, but for reaction — all the more cynical because not veiled by any *mystique,* any illusions. The main impediment that prevented Clemenceau — as well as many other French intellectuals — from advancing beyond radicalism was *rationalism.* This narrow, niggardly, flat rationalism has long since become powerless against the Church, but instead has changed into a staunch armor of thick-headedness against Communist dialectics. I once wrote something about Clemenceau's rationalism; I must look it up.

* * *

Rakovsky was virtually my last contact with the old revolutionary generation. After his capitulation there is nobody left. Even though my correspondence with Rakovsky stopped, for reasons of censorship, at the time of my deportation, nevertheless the image of Rakovsky has remained a symbolic link with my old comrades-in-arms.

Now nobody remains. For a long time now I have not been able to satisfy my need to exchange ideas and discuss problems with someone else. I am reduced to carrying on a dialogue with the newspapers, or rather through the newspapers with facts and opinions.

And still I think that the work in which I am engaged now, despite its extremely insufficient and fragmentary nature, is the most important work of my life — more important than 1917, more important than the period of the Civil War or any other.

For the sake of clarity I would put it this way. Had I not been present in 1917 in Petersburg, the October Revolution would still have taken place — *on the condition that Lenin was present and in command.* If neither Lenin nor I had been present in Petersburg, there would have been no October Revolution: the leadership of the Bolshevik Party would have prevented it from occurring — of this I have not the slightest doubt! If Lenin had not been in Petersburg, I doubt whether I could have managed to overcome the resistance of the Bolshevik leaders. The struggle with "Trotskyism" (i.e., with the proletarian revolution) would have commenced in May, 1917, and the outcome of the revolution would have been in question. But I repeat, granted the presence of Lenin the October Revolution would have been victorious anyway. The same could by and large be said of the Civil War, although in its first period, especially at the time of the fall of Simbirsk and Kazan, Lenin wavered and was beset by doubts. But this was undoubtedly a passing mood which he probably never even admitted to anyone but me.*

Thus I cannot speak of the "indispensability" of my work,

* I must tell about this in greater detail.

even about the period from 1917 to 1921. But now my work is "indispensable" in the full sense of the word. There is no arrogance in this claim at all. The collapse of the two Internationals has posed a problem which none of the leaders of these Internationals is at all equipped to solve. The vicissitudes of my personal fate have confronted me with this problem and armed me with important experience in dealing with it. There is now no one except me to carry out the mission of arming a new generation with the revolutionary method over the heads of the leaders of the Second and Third International. And I am in a complete agreement with Lenin (or rather Turgenev) that the worst vice is to be more than 55 years old! I need at least about five more years of uninterrupted work to ensure the succession.

March 26

In Belgium Spaak has become a minister. A miserable character! Last year he came to see me in Paris to "ask my advice." We discussed in detail, for about two hours, the situation in the Belgian party. I was amazed by his political superficiality. For instance, the idea of working in the trade unions had never occurred to him. "Yes, yes, this is very important!" He took out a pad and began to take notes. "And is this a revolutionary leader?" I thought. All through our conversation Spaak kept "agreeing" and taking notes. But there was a little something in his agreement which made me dubious. Not that he seemed to me insincere. On the contrary, he came with the best intentions: to inform and strengthen himself before the battle. But apparently my formulations frightened him. "Oh, is that so? This is much more serious than I thought . . ." This note sounded in all his responses, even though in words he was "agreeing." In general, he seemed to me to be an honest "friend of the people" from an enlightened bourgeois milieu, no more than that. But *honest* is just the word: he was visibly disgusted by the corruption surrounding Vandervelde-Anseele. Some time later I received a letter from him. The trade unionists were demanding the abandonment of *Action,* threatening to split with the Party. The Central Committee of the Party was willing to yield to this blackmail. Spaak was asking for advice whether to give in or not. I answered that to give in would mean to commit political *hara-kiri.* (Earlier, in our conversation I had reproached Spaak for his submissiveness, especially for his behavior during the Party Congress of 1933 (?), which passed the resolution on "planning." Spaak agreed with this too.) *Action* was saved: after a shameful episode with the cooperative bank, the right had to retreat temporarily. But the behavior of Spaak himself remained throughout vacillating, lacking in confidence, and false. And now this "revolutionary" hero has become the Minister of Transport in the "National Ministry." Shoddy little man!

What was it that decided Spaak — the fear of further action on the part of the masses or petty personal vanity (to become a "minister"!)? In the end, the difference is not great, since these two motives so frequently reinforce each other!

March 27

In 1903 in Paris a performance of Gorky's *The Lower Depths* was organized, the proceeds from which were to benefit *Iskra.* There was talk of giving a part to N., very likely on my initiative. I thought she would play her part well, "sincerely." But nothing came of it, and the part was given to someone else. I was surprised and distressed. Only later I understood that N. cannot "act a part" in any sphere. She always and under all conditions, all her life and in all possible surroundings — and we have changed quite a few of them — has remained true to herself, and has never allowed her surroundings to influence her inner life . . .

Today on our walk we went up a hill. N. got tired and unexpectedly sat down, all pale, on the dry leaves (the earth is still a bit damp). Even now she still walks beautifully, without fatigue, and her gait is quite youthful, like her whole figure. But for the last few months her heart has been acting up now and then. She works too much — with passion, as in everything she undertakes, and today it showed during the steep ascent up the hill. N. sat down all of a sudden — she obviously just *could not* go any further — and smiled apologetically. What a pang of pity I felt for youth, *her* youth . . . One night we ran home from the Paris Opera to the *rue* Gassendi, 46, *au pas gymnastique,* holding hands. It was in 1903. Our combined age was 46 . . . N. was probably the more indefatigable one. Once, while a whole crowd of us were walking somewhere in the outskirts of Paris, we came to a bridge. A steep cement pier sloped down from a great height. Two small boys had climbed on to the pier over the parapet of the bridge and were looking down on the passers-by. Suddenly N. started climbing toward them up the steep smooth slope of the pier. I was petrified. I didn't think it was possible to climb up there. But she kept walking up with her graceful stride, on high heels, smiling to the boys. They waited for her with interest. We all stopped anxiously. N. went all the way up without looking at us, talked to the children, and came down the same way, without having made, as far as one could see, a single superfluous effort or taken a single uncertain step . . . It was spring, and the sun was shining as brightly as it did today when N. suddenly sat down in the grass . . .

"Dagegen ist nun einmal kein Kraut gewachsen," Engels wrote about old age and death. All the events and experiences of life are arranged along this inexorable arch between birth and the grave. This arch constitutes life itself. Without this arch there would be not only no old age, but also no youth. Old age is "necessary" because it has experience and wisdom. Youth, after all, is so beautiful exactly because there is old age and death.

Perhaps all these thoughts come to mind because the radio is playing Wagner's *Götterdämmerung.*

March 29

Some time I must relate how the G.P.U. stole documents out of my archives. But there is no hurry about it . . .

Today in *Le petit Dauphinois* there is a remarkable report from Brussels, actually a slightly veiled interview with De Man. *Le petit D.* is a reactionary newspaper, but so far not a fascist one. It has unlimited sympathy for De Man, or at any rate its Brussels correspondent has. We are told, in any case, that De Man's plan rests on two pillars: the Pope of Rome and the King of Belgium. In the papal encyclical "Quadragesimo Anno," it says that the masters of money can, if they wish, prevent people from breathing. According to De Man, Van Zeeland, the Prime Minister, operates on this principle. Or rather De Man wants Van Zeeland to operate on the principle of this encyclical. The late King, it transpires, regarded the plan with sympathy, and the new King Leopold *"étudiait chaque jour, avec le même intérêt, les travaux d'Henry de Man avant que celui-ci devienne son ministre."* All this was revealed to the correspondent by De Man himself.

As for the plan itself. First: "The state must liberate itself from the tutelage of the banks and take the levers of command in its own hands." Second: corporations à la Mussolini for the administration of things; parliamentary institutions for the governing of people. It is obvious that all this was written at De Man's dictation; no journalist could think up such formulas!

Administration of things and governing of people are plagiarisms from Engels: the withering away of the state will consist, according to Engels, in the gradual replacement of government over persons by the administration of things. But how it is possible to set up two regimes at the same time, one corporative and the other parliamentary, one for things and the other for people — this is beyond comprehension. By what means does De Man propose to separate people from things: i.e., property-owners from their property? For in fact the whole question boils down to that. De Man does not of course want revolutionary expropriation, and no encyclical would induce even the most pious plunderers to place their banks and trusts under the management of impotent "corporations."

This whole scheme — half adventure, half plot against the people — will end in a pitiful collapse, after which both De Man and Spaak will be left with besmirched reputations. The banks, after being saved by them by means of devaluation, will show the innovators how to "liberate" the state from their tutelage!

* * *

In the diplomatic negotiations in Moscow (the visit of Eden, etc.) among many other things, the fate of the Comintern is being settled. If England accepts the idea of a pact (without Germany), the congress of the Comintern promised for the first half of this year will of course not be called. If England and France reach an agreement with Germany (without the U.S.S.R.), the congress will probably be held. But this congress of the bankrupts is not capable of giving anything to the proletariat!

* * *

Claude Farrère, whom I mentioned the other day, has been elected to the Academy. What a revolting pack of old clowns!

Barthou, who, being a bad writer, is of course a member of the Academy also, gave the following reply when asked in a questionnaire, "What would you wish for yourself?": "I have nothing to wish for: in my youth I dreamed about a career as a minister and academician, and in my ripe years I have become both." It is impossible to characterize oneself with greater sarcasm!

[*Clipping pasted in*] The stinking dregs of Trotskyists, Zinovievists, former princes, counts, gendarmes, all this trash, acting as one, are trying to undermine the walls of our state.

This, of course, is from *Pravda*. No Cadets, or Mensheviks, or Socialist Revolutionaries are mentioned — only Trotskyists and princes act "as one." There is something imperviously stupid in this statement, and in the stupidity there is something fatal. Only a historically doomed clique could become so degenerate and moronic!

At the same time, the provocative character of this stupidity brings out two mutually connected circumstances: (1) Something there is out of order, very much out of order; "disorder" lies somewhere deep within the bureaucracy itself, or more correctly within its ruling stratum; the "amalgam" of dregs and trash is directed against some third element, not belonging either to the princes or the Trotskyists — most likely against liberal tendencies within the ranks of the ruling bureaucracy. (2) Some new practical steps against the "Trotskyists" are in preparation as the groundwork for a blow at some closer and more intimate enemies of Stalin's Bonapartism. One might suppose that some new *coup d'état* was being prepared, with the aim of providing juridical sanction for Stalin's personal power. But what could this *coup d'état* consist of? Not a crown, surely? The title of "leader" conferred for life? But that would smack too much of the *Führer!* The "technical" problems of Bonapartism apparently present greater and greater political difficulties. Some new stage is being prepared, by comparison with which Kirov's murder was only an ominous portent.

March 31

Here's a funny story! The Soviet historian V. I. Nevsky is no worse and no better than many another Soviet historian: sloppy, slipshod, dogmatic, but with an admixture of a certain naïveté which — against the general background of "expedient" falsifications — sometimes gives an appearance of scrupulousness. Nevsky belongs to no Opposition groups. Nevertheless he is being systematically hounded. Why? Here is one possible explanation. In his *History of the R*[*ussian*] *C*[*ommunist*] *P*[*arty*], which came out in 1924, in the bibliographical survey Nevsky remarks:

"Booklets like the pamphlet by Konst[antin] [*sic*] Molotov, 'Toward the History of the Party,' not only do not contribute anything, but perhaps do real harm — they contain such a quantity of errors: in the mere 39 pages of this booklet we counted 19 errors! . . ." In 1924 Nevsky had no way of knowing that Molotov's star would rise high and that the "19 errors" of the booklet would not prevent its author from becoming Chairman of the Council of People's Commissars. Molotov has arranged — evidently through the Organizational Bureau, where at one time (a long time ago now!) he was boss — to have poor Nevsky hounded . . . But times change: Molotov's star has dimmed, and — who knows? — Nevsky's remark about the illiteracy of the Chairman of the Council of Commissars might yet bring greater glory to the unlucky historian. Truly it is a funny story! . . .

April 1935

April 2

Eden's negotiations in Moscow have ended with a rather widely broadcast diplomatic communiqué which includes the mutual pledge *not to harm* the interests and well-being of the other party. On his way to Warsaw, Eden indelicately emphasized that this was not only an obligation of Great Britain toward the U.S.S.R. but also an obligation of the U.S.S.R. toward Great Britain. This is an issue concerning China and India, the Comintern, and "Soviet" China. What pledges have been given by Moscow in this respect? It will be possible to verify the nature of the Kremlin's pledges by observing what is done about convoking the Comintern congress in Moscow. A congress without Chinese, Indians and Englishmen is impossible. But after the Moscow negotiations is it possible to hold one with Chinese, Indian and English delegates present?

After all, if Stalin did undertake to liquidate the Comintern secretly, it would be a tremendous gain for the cause of the socialist revolution. But a pledge of this sort would at the same time be an unmistakable proof that the Soviet bureaucracy had definitively broken with the world proletariat.

* * *

Yesterday another period of ill health began for me. Weakness, slightly feverish condition, an extraordinary humming in my ears. Last time, during a similar spell, H. M. was at the local Prefect's. The latter inquired about me, and learning that I was sick, exclaimed in genuine alarm: "This is extremely unpleasant, extremely unpleasant! . . . If he dies here, why, we will not be able to bury him under his assumed name!" Everyone has his worries!

* * *

I have just received a letter from Paris. Aleksandra Lvovna Sokolovskaya, my first wife, who was living in Leningrad with our grandchildren, has been deported to Siberia. A postcard from her has already been received abroad, sent from Tobolsk, where she is staying *en route* to more distant parts of Siberia. The letters from our younger son, Seryozha, professor in the Institute of Technology, have stopped. In the last one he wrote that certain disturbing rumors were gathering around him. Obviously he too has been deported from Moscow. I don't think that Al. Lvovna has been politically at all active during the last few years, both because of her age and the three children on her hands. Several weeks ago in *Pravda,* in an article devoted to the fight against "remnants" and "dregs," the name of A. L. was also mentioned — in the usual hoodlum manner — but only in passing; she was accused of having exerted a harmful influence — in 1931! — on a group of students — I think in the Institute of Forestry. *Pravda* could not discover any later crimes. But the very mention of her name was by itself an unmistakable sign that we must expect a blow in this direction too.

Platon Volkov, the husband of my late daughter Zinushka, has been arrested again, though he was already in exile, and sent further on. Sevushka (my grandson), the little son of Platon and Zina, who is now eight years old, has only recently moved from Vienna to Paris. He was with his mother in Berlin during the last period of her life. She took her own life while Seva was away at school. He settled for a short time with my older son and daughter-in-law. But they were obliged to leave Germany hastily because of the evident approach of a fascist regime. Sevushka was taken to Vienna to avoid an unnecessary change in the language. There some old friends of ours arranged for his schooling. After we had moved to France, we decided, with the beginning of counterrevolutionary upheavals in Austria, to transfer the boy to Paris, to live with my older son and daughter-in-law. But the seven-year-old Sevushka was persistently refused a visa. Arrangements took many a long month. Only recently did we succeed in getting him there. During his stay in Vienna Seva has completely forgotten his Russian and French. And how beautifully he used to speak Russian, with the singsong Moscow accent, when at the age of five he first came to us in Prinkipo with his mother! There, in the kindergarten, he quickly learned French and some Turkish. In Berlin he switched to German and in Vienna became a real German; and now, in a Parisian school, he is switching back to French. He knows about the death of his mother, and from time to time inquires about "Platosha" (his father), who has become a myth for him.

My younger son, Seryozha, in contrast to the older one, and partly out of direct opposition to him, from the age of 12 or so turned his back on politics; he practiced gymnastics, loved the circus, and even wanted to become a circus performer; later he took up technical subjects, worked hard, and became a professor; recently in collaboration with two other engineers he published a book on motors. If he has really been banished, it is entirely for reasons of personal revenge; there could be no political basis for it.

As an illustration of living conditions in Moscow. Seryozha married early: he and his wife lived for several years in one room which was left to them in the last apartment we occupied after leaving the Kremlin. About a year and a half ago Seryozha and his wife were separated, but for lack of another room they continued to live together until very recently. Probably it has taken the G.P.U. to separate them by sending them in different directions. Perhaps Lelia has been deported too? It is not impossible.

April 3

I obviously underestimated the *immediate* practical meaning of the pronouncement about the "dregs of the Trotskyists." (See March 30.) The knife-blade of "political action" is once again pointed toward people personally close to me. Last night, when I handed N. the letter from our older son, from Paris, she said: "They will not deport him [Seryozha] under any circumstances; they will torture him in order to get something out of him, and after that they will destroy him."

Evidently the deportation to Siberia of 1,074 people was a deliberate pretext for new measures against the Opposition.* The "counts, gendarmes and princes" represent only the first half of the amalgam, its foundation. But it would be better to quote a more complete excerpt from *Pravda:*

[*Newspaper clipping pasted in.*]

We must take really effective measures against the machinations of our enemies. Because of Oblomovism, gullibility, because of

* A comparison of the documents does not confirm this supposition.

opportunistic complacency toward anti-Party elements and enemies acting under the direction of foreign intelligence services, these elements at times succeed in penetrating our Party organization.

The dregs of Zinovievists, Trotskyists, former princes, counts, and gendarmes — all this trash, acting as one, are trying to undermine the walls of our state. [*The words "under the direction of foreign intelligence services" and "acting as one" are underlined in pencil.*]

[*The following clipping is scored over diagonally several times.*] Recent exposures of anti-Party elements and the recent report of the People's Commissariat for Internal Affairs on the arrest, deportation, and prosecution of former tsarist high officials in Leningrad show that there are still political and criminal swindlers ready to crawl through any crack.

Recently in Moscow there was a trial of a shady speculator named Shaposhnik who traveled around from city to city and passed himself off everywhere as an engineer. Certain nincompoops gave him jobs, entrusted state property to him, and it took quite a considerable time before he was exposed and put in prison. Or another adventurer and enemy named Krasovsky, alias Zagorodny, who represented himself as a candidate-member of the Central Executive Committee. Certain imbeciles took him at his word, and he penetrated as far as membership in an election commission and there committed a crime. In the Saratov district a spy [*this word is underlined in pencil*], using an absurd set of forged papers, wormed his way into a responsible job and only some time later was caught and shot.

(*Pravda,* March 25).

To whom do the words "foreign intelligence services" refer? To the princes or to Trotskyists? *Pravda* adds that they act "as one." The reason for linking them together, in any case, is to give the G.P.U. a chance to prosecute "Trotskyists" and "Zinovievists" as agents of foreign intelligence services. This is quite obvious.

Here is the initial announcement about the 1,074:

[*Clipping pasted in. The words "for the benefit of foreign States" are underlined in pencil. The entire clipping is bracketed and the figure 1074 written in the margin.*] During the last few days a group of citizens consisting of former aristocrats, high tsarist officials, big capitalists, landowners, gendarmes, tsarist policemen, and others have been arrested and deported to the Eastern regions of the U.S.S.R. for violating the place-of-residence rules and the passport law. Of these there were: former princes — 41; former counts — 33; former barons — 76; former large manufacturers — 35; former big landowners — 68; former big commercial capitalists — 19; former high tsarist officials from tsarist ministries — 142; former generals and former officers of the tsarist and White armies — 547; former high-ranking officials of the gendarmerie, police and Okhrana —113.

Some of those deported have been prosecuted by organs of public supervision for actions against the Soviet state and for the benefit of foreign states.

(*Pravda,* March 20)

In this there is as yet not a word about the Trotskyists; the charge of acting for the benefit of the foreign states is made so far only against the former "princes and gendarmes." Only five days later *Pravda* reports that the Trotskyists and Zinovievists were acting "as one" with them. Such is the crude technique of the "amalgam."

* * *

With what immediacy and perspicacity N. imagined Seryozha in prison: he must suffer doubly, since his interests are quite outside of politics, and indeed he is completely an innocent bystander suffering for deeds not his own [*literally:* "having a hangover after someone else's feast"]. N. even recalled Barychkin: "He will take revenge on him now!" Barychkin is a former worker from Mytishchensk (a town near Moscow) who has been thoroughly corrupted and depraved in the G.P.U. I think that in 1924 he was caught in an embezzlement, and Yagoda "saved" him and thus made him his slave. At one time this Barychkin used to accompany me frequently on my hunting and fishing trips and to amaze me by his mixture of revolutionary fervor, buffoonery and servility. The longer I knew him, the more antipathetic he became, and I got rid of him. He complained whiningly to N. I. Muralov: "L. D. does not take me hunting any more . . ." After this, as I said, he was caught in an embezzlement, and as a pardoned criminal ostentatiously demonstrated his hatred for the Opposition in order to justify the confidence of the authorities.

When I was being deported from Moscow he entered my apartment impudently, without taking off his coat and hat. "What are you doing with your hat on?" I said to him. He went out without saying anything, with the look of a whipped dog. At the station, when the G.P.U. men were carrying me in their arms, Lyova shouted, "Look, workers, at the way they are carrying Trotsky!" Barychkin leapt at him and started to cover his mouth with his hand. Seryozha struck Barychkin hard on the face. The latter jumped back muttering something, but did not raise a row . . . This is what N. was thinking about when she said, "He will remind Seryozha of that now . . ."

April 4

All the current *"misères"* of our personal lives have receded into the background in the face of our anxiety for Seryozha, A. L. [Sokolovskaya], and the children. I said to N. yesterday: "It seems now that our life before we got the last letter from Lyova was almost beautiful and serene . . ." N. behaves with great fortitude, for my sake, but she feels all this immeasurably more deeply than I do.

The motive of *personal revenge* has always been a considerable factor in the repressive policies of Stalin. Kamenev told me how the three of them — Stalin, Kamenev, and Dzherzhinsky — in Zubalovo, in the summer of 1923 (or 1924?) spent the day in a "heart-to-heart" conversation over wine. They were bound together by their campaign against me, which had recently been initiated. After the wine, on the balcony, the talk touched upon a sentimental subject — personal tastes and predilections, something of that sort. Stalin said, "The greatest delight is to mark one's enemy, prepare everything, avenge oneself thoroughly, and then go to sleep."

His craving for revenge on me is completely unsatisfied: there have been, so to speak, physical blows, but morally nothing has been achieved. There is no refusal to work, no "repentance," no isolation; on the contrary, a new historical momentum has been acquired which it is already impossible to halt. This is the source of gravest apprehensions for Stalin: that savage fears ideas, since he knows their explosive power and knows his own weakness in the face of them. At the same time he is clever enough to realize that even today I would not change places with him: hence the psychology of a man stung. But if revenge on a higher plane has not succeeded — and clearly it will not succeed — it is still possible to reward oneself with police blows against people close to me. Naturally, Stalin would not hesitate a moment to organize an attempt on my life, but he is afraid of the political consequences: the accusation will undoubtedly fall on him. Blows against my inti-

Лева переслал открытку А. Львовны уже с места ссылки. Тот же отчетливый, слегка детский почерк, и то же отсутствие жалоб...

Отправлено [illegible] — Леве.

30/III-35

Дорогой Лева, Ваше письмо от 3/III переслали мне сюда, и я только на днях его получила. Как я рада за Севушку! Надеюсь, что он уже с Вами, и что, наконец, его существование войдет в нормальное русло. Бедный мальчонок, теперь ему нужно приспособляться к новому языку. Карточку его мне тоже переслали. Он очевидно очень вытянулся. Надеюсь Вы получили мое письмо из Тобольска, где я временно находилась. Теперь я уже нахожусь на месте постоянного жительства — С. Демьянск, Уватского района, Омской обл. Вернулись ли к Вам деньги, которые я не успела получить? От детишек получаю письма, но ясного представления о их жизни не имею. Вере с ними, без меня, вероятно, приходится довольно трудно; хотя она меня все успокаивает. Мое здоровье сносно. Врача здесь нет, а потому необходимо быть здоровой. Жду дальнейших вестей о Севушке.

Будьте здоровы. Целую. Ваша,

Алекс—

PARIS-RP 12 10 IV 1935

"The same clear, slightly childish handwriting . . ."

(April 9)

1935

8 мая. Из Москвы через Париж сообщают: «Вам уже конечно писали по поводу их маленьких неприятностей». Речь идет явно о Сереже (и его подруге). Но нам ничего не писали, вернее письмо погибло в пути, как большинство писем, даже совершенно невинных. Что значит „маленькие" неприятности? По какому масштабу „маленькие"? От самого Сережи вестей нет...

Старость есть самая неожиданная из всех вещей, какие случаются с человеком.

Норвежское рабочее правительство, как будто твердо обещало визу. Придется, видимо, ею воспользоваться. Дальнейшее пребывание во Франции здесь связано со все большими трудностями, притом в обоих вариантах: в случае непрерывного продвижения реакции, как и в случае успешного развития революционного движения. Не имея возможности взять меня в другую стра-

"Old age is the most unexpected of all the things that happen to a man."

(May 8)

Письмо Н. И. Троцкой о сыне

За последнее время в среде товарищей довольно широко распространились слухи, что Сталин, на этот раз в качестве орудия мести, избрал нашего младшего сына Сергея. Друзья запрашивают нас: верно ли это? Это верно: Да, Сережа арестован в самом начале этого года. Если в первое время можно было еще надеяться на то, что арест случайный, и что сына не сегодня-завтра освободят, то сейчас уже очевидно, что намерения арестовавших гораздо серьезнее. Так как многие из товарищей живо интересуются новым ударом, постигшим нашу семью, то будет может быть лучше, если я расскажу, как обстоит дело в письме, предназначенном для общего сведения.

Сережа родился в 1909 г. Он встретил октябрьскую революцию восьмилетним мальчиком и рос в Кремле. В семьях, где старшие поглощены политикой, младшие члены нередко отталкиваются от политики. Так было и у нас. Сережа никогда не занимался политическими вопросами и не был даже членом Комсомола.

"Seryozha was arrested . . ."

(June 1)

лось бы неизменным. Я умру пролетарским революционером, марксистом, диалектическим материалистом и, следовательно, непримиримым атеистом. Моя вера в коммунистическое будущее человечества сейчас не менее горяча, но более крепка, чем в дни моей юности.

Наташа подошла сейчас со двора к окну и раскрыла его шире, чтоб воздух свободнее проникал в мою комнату. Я вижу яркую зеленую полосу травы под стеной, чистое голубое небо над стеной и солнечный свет везде. Жизнь прекрасна. Пусть грядущие поколения очистят ее от зла, гнета, насилия и наслаждаются ею вполне.

27 февраля 1940. Л. Троцкий

Койоакан

"Life is beautiful."

(The Testament)

mates in Russia cannot give him the necessary "satisfaction," and at the same time they cause serious political inconveniences. To announce that Seryozha worked "under the direction of foreign intelligence services"? It's too incongruous; the motive of personal revenge would be revealed too directly; it would be too compromising for Stalin personally.

* * *

[*Newspaper clipping pasted in.*]

L'U.R.S.S. se serait engagée
à mettre fin à la propagande communiste
en Grande-Bretagne et dans les dominions.

Londres, 3 avril. — Au cours de ses récents entretiens avec M. Eden, M. Litvinoff, commissaire soviétique aux affaires étrangères, aurait informé le lord du Sceau privé de la décision du gouvernement de Moscou, de mettre un terme à la propagande communiste en Grande-Bretagne et dans les dominions.

Il semble que les fonds, destinés à cette propagande, aient été progressivement supprimés au cours de ses derniers mois.

This looks very much like the truth. Litvinov — one should do him justice — for a long time now has regarded the Comintern as an unprofitable and harmful institution. Deep in his heart Stalin agrees with him. The item about the progressive reduction of the subsidies from month to month is very expressive. The Kremlin has planned a definite "liquidation" period for each party. To be sure, the sections of the Comintern will not disappear even after this period, but they will be greatly curtailed and will have to adjust their mode of existence to a new budget. Along with this, personal regroupings, resignations, desertions and denunciations are to be expected. A considerable number of the "leaders," journalists, and propagandists of the Comintern represent a pure type of the *fromagiste,* the bread-and-butter man: if there is no pay, then there is no more loyalty either.

The turn to the *right* in the sphere of both foreign and domestic politics forces Stalin to strike out at the *left* with all his might: this is his insurance against an opposition. But it is an absolutely unreliable insurance. The change in the whole social order and way of life in the U.S.S.R. must inevitably produce a new acute political convulsion.

* * *

It is hard right now to work on my book on Lenin: my thoughts simply don't want to concentrate on the year 1893! The weather has changed sharply in the last few days. Although the gardens are in bloom, it has been snowing today since early morning; everything was covered with a white shroud; then it melted; now it is snowing again but melting right away. The sky is gray; from the mountains the fog is creeping down into the valley; in the house it is chilly and damp. N. is fussing over the housework with a heavy weight in her heart. Life is not an easy matter . . . You cannot live through it without falling into prostration and cynicism unless you have before you a great idea which raises you above personal misery, above weakness, above all kinds of perfidy and baseness.

* * *

I read yesterday a novel by Victor Margueritte called *Le Compagnon.* A very feeble writer; in his banal prose one feels no trace of the great school of the French novel. His radical leanings are superficial and sentimental. This radicalism — with a lining of feminism — might not have looked bad in the age of Louis-Philippe. Now it seems completely soured. The eroticism of the novel smacks of the police blotter.

April 5

Nevertheless Mar[gueritte]'s novel does throw some light on personal and family relations in certain — and by no means the worst — bourgeois circles in France. The "hero" of the novel is a socialist. The author reproaches his hero for adopting the attitude toward women of a "bourgeois" — or rather, one should say, of a slave-owner. The polemic in *Le Populaire* on the subject of whether or not to give the franchise to women demonstrates that among the socialists, too, there reigns the same base proprietary attitude toward women that permeates the legislation and law of the country.

But even Margueritte's proposals for emancipation actually do not go beyond a separate checkbook for the wife. While in our uncouth Russia there is much barbarism, almost zoologism, in the old bourgeois cultures there are horrible encrustations of fossilized narrow-mindedness, crystallized cruelty, polished cynicism . . . What enormous upheavals, transformations, and efforts will yet be needed to raise the average man to a higher level of personality!

The weather is the same. A cold sleet is falling from the sky. The gardens are in bloom. The fruit harvest will suffer greatly this year.

We do not receive our mail here. The big mail is brought from Paris whenever opportunity arises (about twice a month); extremely urgent letters go via an intermediate address and arrive with some delay. Now we are awaiting news of Seryozha — N. especially, and her inner life is spent in this expectation. But it is not simple to get reliable information. Correspondence with Seryozha, even in more auspicious times, was a lottery. I did not write to him at all, so as not to give the authorities any reason for harassing him. N. was the only one who wrote, and even then only about personal things. Seryozha answered the same way. There have been long periods when letters would stop coming altogether. Then, all of a sudden, a postcard would come through, and the correspondence would be resumed for a time. After the latest events (the murder of Kirov, etc.) the censorship of correspondence with foreign countries must have become even harsher. If Seryozha is in prison, he will not be allowed to write abroad, of course. If he has already been deported, the situation may be somewhat more favorable, but still everything depends on the concrete circumstances. During the last few months of their deportation the Rakovskys were completely isolated from the outside world: not a single letter, even from their closest relatives, reached them. Some one of those near to me might have written about Seryozha's arrest. But who? No one is left, evidently . . . And even if someone sympathetic to me is left, he would not know the address.

* * *

The rain has stopped. N. and I went walking between 4 and 5 o'clock in the afternoon . . . Quiet and comparatively gentle weather, the sky overcast; a veil of fog over the mountains, the smell of manure in the air. "March looked like April, and now April has become March." These are N.'s words; somehow I let such observations slip by me unless N. calls my attention to them. Her voice made me feel a sudden pang in my heart. Her voice, slightly hoarse, comes from deep in her chest. When she suffers it withdraws even deeper, as if her soul were speaking directly. How well I know this voice of tenderness and suffering! After a long interval N. spoke about Seryozha again. "What can they demand from him? That he confess? But he has nothing to confess. That he 'renounce' his father? In what sense? But for the very reason that he has nothing to confess, he has no sense of perspective. How long will they hold him?"

N. recalled how after a meeting of the Politburo (this was in 1926) some friends of that period were in our apartment awaiting the results. I came in with Pyatakov (as a member of the Central Committee Pyatakov had the right to attend meetings of the Politburo). Very much disturbed, Pyatakov told about the course of "events." I had said at the meeting that Stalin had finally entered his candidacy for the post of the gravedigger of the Party and the Revolution . . . Stalin, as a protest, had left the meeting. On the motion of the disconcerted Rykov and Rudzutak, I was "censured." While telling about this, Pyatakov turned toward me and said with emphasis, "He will never forgive you for this: neither you, nor your children, nor your grandchildren." At that time, as N. recalled, the words about my children and grandchildren seemed remote, rather a mere turn of phrase. But there we are — it reached my children and even my grandchildren: they have been torn away from A. L. — what will become of them? And the older one, Lyovushka, is already 15 . . .

We spoke about Seryozha. In Prinkipo the question of his moving abroad was discussed. But where and how? Lyova has politics in his blood, and this justifies his emigration. But Seryozha's ties are with technology and the Institute. He would have pined away in Prinkipo. Furthermore, it was hard to foresee the future: when would a break come in the course of events? In what direction? And if something happened to me abroad? We were afraid to tear Seryozha away from his "roots." Zinushka was brought abroad to take a cure — and even that ended tragically.

N. is haunted by the thought of what a heavy heart Seryozha must have in prison (if he is in prison). Perhaps he may think that we have somehow forgotten about him, left him to his fate. If he is in a concentration camp, what can he hope for? He cannot behave better than he did as a young professor in his Institute . . .

"Perhaps they had simply forgotten about him in the last few years, and have now suddenly recalled that they possess such a treasure, and have decided to construct a big new case with it . . ." These, again, are Natasha's thoughts. She asked me if I thought that Stalin knows about the case. I answered that he never overlooks such "cases," that his specialty actually consists in "cases" like this.

For the last two days, N. has thought more about A. L. than about Seryozha: it may be, after all, that Seryozha is not in any trouble, but A. L. at 60 years of age has been sent somewhere to the far North.

* * *

The depth and strength of a human character are defined by its moral *reserves*. People reveal themselves completely only when they are thrown out of the customary conditions of their life, for only then do they have to fall back on their reserves. N. and I have been together for almost 33 years (a third of a century!), and in tragic hours I am always amazed at the reserves of her character . . . Whether because our strength is declining, or for some other reason, but I should very much like to fix N.'s image on paper, at least partially.

* * *

I have finished a novel by Léon Frapié, *La Maternelle,* a popular edition at 2 francs. I don't know this author at all. In any case he shows very courageously the back yard — and the darkest corner of the back yard — of French civilization, of Paris. The cruelty and meanness of life strike hardest at the children, at the very smallest ones. Frapié, then, set himself a problem of looking at present-day civilization through the frightened eyes of the hungry maltreated children with hereditary vices in their blood. The narrative is not sustained artistically; there are breakdowns and failures; the heroine's arguments are at times naïve and even mannered; but the author succeeds in creating the necessary impression. He knows of no way out and does not even seem to be looking for one. The book is charged with hopelessness. But this hopelessness is immeasurably higher than the smug and cheap recipes of Victor Margueritte.

* * *

Here is the headline of *L'Humanité* for April 4th:

[*Newspaper clipping pasted in.*]

"LE GOUVERNEMENT DOIT INTERDIRE LA MOBILISATION ROUGE DU 7 AVRIL."

("AMI DU PEUPLE," 1-ER AVRIL)

LE LENDEMAIN, LE MINISTRE RADICAL RÉGNIER OBÉIT. "NOTRE PROTESTATION A ÉTÉ ENTENDUE."

("AMI DU PEUPLE," 3 AVRIL)

CONCLUSION: LE GOUVERNEMENT EST AUX ORDRES DES FASCISTES!

Mais ce n'est pas leur dernière "conclusion," ils en ont une autre: "exigeons plus que jamais la dissolution et le désarmement des Ligues fascistes . . ." par le gouvernement qui est aux ordres des fascistes! Nothing will save these people!

April 7

[*The following are newspaper clippings pasted in against the entry for April 7.*]

M. HENRI DORGÈRES SE DÉFEND D'AVOIR DANS SES PROPOS TENUS EN PUBLIC OFFENSÉ LE CODE

Il reste d'ailleurs très confiant dans l'issue des poursuites engagées contre lui.

Rouen, 11 avril. — M. Henri Dorgères, président du comité de défense paysanne du Nord-Ouest, est arrivé à Rouen, ce matin, et a comparu devant M. Leroy, juge d'instruction.

Celui-ci a procédé, en présence de M. Dorgères, à la levée des scellés et a commencé le dépouillement des dossiers saisis. M. Dorgères a été interrogé sur les faits. Il a répondu qu'il était prêt à répéter les paroles prononcées par lui dans les réunions publiques car elles n'avaient rien qui puisse motiver son inculpation.

— J'ai demandé notamment aux paysans, a dit M. Dorgères: "Nous pourrions être appelés à vous demander de faire la grève de l'impôt. Seriez-vous prêts à répondre oui?"

L'interrogatoire a été suspendu à midi pour reprendre à 14 h., mais à ce moment M. Dorgères a mandaté son secrétaire, M. Lefebvre, pour assister à l'ouverture des scellés, lui-même devant se rendre à Paris, où il prendra part, ce soir, à une conférence au Faubourg.

M. Dorgères, que nous avons rencontré au moment où il quittait le Palais de justice, accompagné de M. Suplice, président du comité de défense paysanne de la Seine-Inférieure, et de M. Lefebvre, secrétaire général du même comité, nous a déclaré:

— Je suis très tranquille sur l'issue de l'instruction, car on ne peut trouver dans les dossiers saisis ou dans les paroles que j'ai prononcées dans les réunions publiques, rien qui puisse motiver des poursuites.

Une conférence de M. Henri Dorgères sur la paysannerie française

Paris, 5 avril. — Au théâtre des Ambassadeurs, M. Henri Dorgères donnait, cet après-midi, une conférence sur la paysannerie française.

On connait la campagne que mène M. Dorgères dans les milieux paysans, campagne illustrée par sa candidature à la récente élection législative de Blois. "Le paysan sauvera la France", tel est le thème qu'a développé le conférencier en s'attachant à démontrer que les paysans représentent la partie de la nation qui est restée saine, "celle qui n'a pas connu dans la période d'après-guerre les plaisirs faciles, les dancings et les huit heures", et pour laquelle rien n'a été fait, assure-t-il, par les gouvernements successifs.

M. Dorgères a fait l'apologie de la classe paysanne et une critique acerbe du régime parlementaire, des parlementaires et de l'Etat, dont il demande la réforme au nom du corporatisme et de la famille.

Le programme agricole du Front Paysan

Tours, 6 avril. — A l'issue d'une réunion organisée cet aprés-midi, à Tours, par le Front Paysan, sous la présidence de M. Dorgères, un ordre du jour a été voté, disant notamment:

"Six mille agriculteurs réunis à Tours, devant l'aggravation persistante de la crise, proclament leur volonté de poursuivre une politique basée sur le programme suivant:

"1° Défense et extension de la propriété individuelle et spécialement de la petite propriété paysanne;

"2° Lutte contre l'excès de mesures étatistes et des charges fiscales;

"3° Lutte contre les trusts;

"4° Organisation professionnelle solidement charpentée;

"5° Revalorisation des produits agricoles.

"Ils demandent aux pouvoirs publics:

"a) D'avoir une politique économique qui permette à tous les travailleurs, y compris ceux de la terre, de vivre de leur labeur;

"b) De consulter la représentation agricole, chaque fois que les intérêts de la profession seront en jeu et spécialement lors des négociations des traités de commerce et protestent contre les récentes lois dites d'assainissement des marchés.

The bourgeois press is advertising Dorgères. The path he is following is the surest way to prepare a fascist dictatorship. People like Dorgères will undermine the feeble parliamentary practices of gentlemen like Chautemps in the provinces, and then somebody — perhaps that same De la Rocque (who is in no wise worse than Badinguet) — will deal the final blow to the parliamentary republic.

Regionalism is a response to the diversity of agrarian conditions in France. The provincial fascist and prefascist programs will be as varied and contradictory as are the interests of the different categories — the vine growers, truck gardeners, wheat growers — as well as the different social strata of the peasantry. But all these programs will have in common their hatred of the bank, the treasury, the trust, and the legislators.

The idiots and cowards of the Comintern propose as their substitute for this profound movement a program of "partial demands" badly copied from old school notebooks.

April 9

The election in Danzig supplemented the lesson provided by the Saar plebiscite. The Nazis got "only" 60%; here there was no question of annexation to Germany. The Nazi terror in Danzig was greater than in the Saar; this demonstrates that terror alone is not decisive. The Social Democrats all but kept the votes they had received in 1933 (38,000), and so did the Catholics (31,000). The Communists dropped from 14,566 to 8,990! In the Saar it was impossible to distinguish the different votes of these parties. The Danzig lesson is thus especially important! The Communists have lost more than a third, while the Social Democrats remain on their previous level. When a revolution is approaching, the extreme party is the one that gains most. After the suppression of a revolution it is the extreme party that loses the most. Under present conditions the Danzig election confirms the progressive paralysis of the Comintern.

[*The following are newspaper clippings pasted in.*]

Dantzig, 8 avril. — Voici les résultats officiels provisoires des élections:

La diminution des suffrages communistes s'explique avant tout par le fait que c'est contre le P. C. qu'a été dirigée essentiellement la terreur nazie et que notre Parti a été réduit pratiquement à l'illégalité.

Les nationaux-socialistes ont obtenu 139.043 suffrages, contre 109.729 le 28 [?] mai 1933.

Les sociaux-démocrates: 38.015 contre 37.882.

Les communistes: 7.990, contre 14.566.

Le centre catholique: 31.525, contre 31.336.

Les nationaux allemands: 9.691 contre 13.596.

Les Polonais: 8.310, contre 6.743.

Les anciens combattants oppositionels: 382.

Sur 250.498 électeurs inscrits, dont 13.000 venus de l'étranger, on compte 234.956 suffrages valables, soit une proportion d'environ 95%, contre 92% en 1933.

La liste nationale-socialiste a donc réuni moins de 60% des suffrages et n'a pas atteint son objectif des deux tiers qui lui seraient nécessaires pour modifier la Constitution dantzikoise.

L'AVANCE COMMUNISTE

[*"9/IV" inserted in longhand*]

	Communistes	S.F.I.O.
1928	3.501	8.395
1932	4.647	6.865
1934	5.218	5.571
1935	6.240	5.462

dans le canton de Carvin

EN TROIS MOIS LA C. G. T. U. A RECRUTÉ 10.000 ADHÉRENTS NOUVEAUX

[*The above is underlined in ink.*]

L'Huma 9/IV

Very important data!!!

Un candidat de Flandin battu par un agrarien dans l'Yonne

Dans le canton de Vézelay (Yonne) le candidat agraire, Mary-Gallot, a été élu dimanche conseiller d'arrondissement par 890 voix contre 648 au candidat de l'Alliance démocratique, Costac, patronné par Flandin.

Le président du conseil est conseiller général de ce même canton et le résultat d'avant-hier ne lui est donc pas précisement favorable.

[*This clipping is crossed over, the word "agrarien" is underlined; "L'Huma 9/IV" written in ink on the clipping, and the following on the margin:*

Selon L'Huma Gallot représente le "front commun."]

Several days ago I read a number of *Vérité:* "Où va La

France?" This paper, as the French say, *se réclame de Trotsky.* There is much that is true in their analysis, but much is left unsaid. I don't know who is writing this series for them. At any rate, it is somebody versed in Marxism.

L'Huma 9/IV

[*Enclosure, the following page, is pasted in.*]

AVANT STRESA

KARL RADEK PROCÈDE À L'ANALYSE DU PROJET DE PACT EUROPÉEN

Moscou, 8 avril. — La presse soviétique consacre de larges commentaires à la préparation de la conférence de Stresa. Parmi les articles publiés ce matin il convient de mentionner celui dans lequel Karl Radek procède à l'analyse critique du projet de pacte dit "européen" qui d'après M. Laval devrait se substituer aux pactes régionaux.

Après avoir rappelé que toute décision prise à Stresa concernant l'U.R.S.S. n'aura de valeur que dans la mesure où l'U.R.S.S. sera conviée à l'approuver, Radek présente les observations suivantes:

1° En cas d'aggression en Europe, il serait puéril et dangereux d'attendre et de s'en remettre au jugement de la Société des Nations, comme semble le préconiser le projet en préparation. "Il faut s'agir," écrit Radek.

[*The last sentence is underlined in pencil.* "Exactly!" *is written in pen on the margin beside this paragraph.*]

2° Le pacte aérien prévoit à l'occident une sanction automatique et immédiate. Or, poursuit Radek, le danger de l'aviation ennemie, si nettement prévu à l'Ouest de l'Europe, serait-il moindre à l'Est, et la rapidité du coup qui pourrait être porté à l'U.R.S.S. serait-elle moins grande?

QUELQUES CONTRADICTIONS

3° Comment peut-on espérer que toutes les nations réunies dans la S. D. N. acceptent, en cas de conflit, de concourir au réétablissement de la sécurité sur un point menacé de l'Europe?

4° Croit-on que l'Allemagne et la Pologne, qui, pour refuser ou éluder le pacte oriental, ont fait valoir qu'elles ne désiraient pas risquer d'être entrainées dans le règlement d'un conflit étranger à leur intérêts quelles ne voulaient pas du passage de troupes étrangères sur leur territoire national, changeraient de point de vue le jour où un pacte universel remplacerait le pacte oriental?

5° Enfin, quel intérêt peut avoir un semblable pacte, alors que la Grande-Bretagne, comme le laisse entendre clairement la presse anglaise, n'y participerait pas?

POUR LE PACTE DE L'EST

Le seul résultat des interminables palabres nécessaires pour mettre au point un pacte européen, ajoute Radek, sera de donner le temps aux pays ennemis de l'ordre en Europe de compléter leur préparation militaire et de préparer une aggression.

L'orateur conclut ainsi:

["Remarkable!" *in the margin. "Aux pays ennemis de l'ordre en Europe" and "l'orateur" underlined in pencil.*]

"L'U.R.S.S. poursuivra la réalisation de pactes régionaux groupant autour d'elle tous ceux que la politique de l'au-[*cut off*]che exaspère et qui se terrent au [*cut off*]

Londres, 9 avril — Quel tableau les satiristes du 21° siècle pourront brosser de notre époque, s'est écrié M. Baldwin, lord président du Conseil, dans le discours qu'il a prononcé, hier soir à Llandrinod (Pays de Galles).

Les grandes puissances leur apparaitront comme des malades des suites de la guerre, des malades dont la convalescence aura été sans cesse interrompue et coupée de rechutes. Personne n'a voulu se soumettre à la grande opération: le désarmement. Par contre, un remède a été pire que le mal: le nationalisme économique.

Certains ont même essayé une médication radicale appelée dictature. Alors traverser l'Europe, cela aura été comme si l'on marchait dans les cours d'une maison de fous.

Dans l'universel bouleversement l'Angleterre apparait au lord président du Conseil comme le seul pays quit ait su garder tout son équilibre:

— Nous n'avons pas rompu avec nos traditions, dit-il. Notre roi est toujours sur un trône, chef et servant de son peuple; nous avons évité la révolution, le sang, la tyrannie et les persécutions.

Notre sens de l'humour nous a permis d'écarter loin de nous certains espèces de visionnaires que sévissaient ailleurs.

[*The first three paragraphs are marked off in the margin with a vertical line; the words* "maison de fous" *are underlined; a black line runs across the last paragraph.*]

Conservative British blockheads in . . . the madhouse of Europe!

Lyova forwarded a postcard from Al. Lvovna, sent from her place of exile. The same clear, slightly childish handwriting, and the same absence of complaints . . .

30/III/35

Dear Lyova, your letter of 3/III was forwarded to me here, and I received it only a few days ago. I am so happy for Sevushka! I hope that he is already with you, and that finally his existence will enter a normal channel. Poor youngster, now he will have to adjust to a new language. His photograph was also forwarded to me. Evidently he has grown much taller. I hope that you got my letter from Tobolsk, where I was living temporarily. Now I am already at a place of permanent residence — S. Demiansk, Uvatsk district, Omsk region, house of Purtova. Was the money, which I did not manage to receive in time, returned to you? I receive letters from the little ones, but don't have a clear idea of their life. My sister is probably having a hard time with them, without me, although she keeps reassuring me. My health is so-so. There is no doctor here, so that I must keep well. I am awaiting further news of Sevushka.

Keep well. Love,

Yours,

Aleks . . .

[*Postcard pasted in. On the reverse:*]

France Paris

[*Line crossed out*]

Poste restante

Rue de Louvre

[*Written alongside:* "Postcard written by A. L. to my son Lyova"]

April 9

The White press at one time hotly debated the question of who it was that ordered the execution of the Tsar's family. The liberals, it seemed, inclined to the opinion that the Ural Executive Committee, being cut off from Moscow, had acted independently. That is not correct. The resolution was adopted in Moscow. The affair took place during a very critical period of the Civil War, when I was spending almost all my time at the front, and my recollections about the case of the Tsar's family are rather fragmentary. I shall relate here what I remember.

During one of my short visits to Moscow — I think a few weeks before the execution of the Romanovs — I incidentally mentioned in the Politburo that, considering the bad situation in the Urals, it would be expedient to accelerate the Tsar's trial. I proposed that we hold an open court trial which would reveal a picture of the whole reign, with its peasant policy, labor policy, national minority and cultural policies, its two wars, etc. The proceedings of the trial would be broadcast throughout the country by radio; (?) [*the question mark is written in above the line*] in the *volosts* [districts including several villages], accounts of the proceedings would be read and commented upon every day. Lenin replied to the effect that it would be very good if it were feasible. But . . . there might not be enough time . . . No debate took place, since I did not insist on my proposal, being absorbed in other work. And in the Politburo, as I remember, there were just three or four of us: Lenin, myself, Sverdlov . . . Kamenev, as I recall, was not there. At that period Lenin was in a rather gloomy mood and did not feel very confident that we would succeed in building an army . . . My next visit to Moscow took place after the fall of Ekaterinburg. Talking to Sverdlov, I asked in passing: "Oh yes, and where is the Tsar?" "It's all over," he answered, "he has been shot." "And where is the family?" "And the family along with him." "All of them?" I asked, apparently with a touch of surprise. "All of them!" replied Sverdlov, "What about it?" He was waiting to see my reaction. I made no reply. "And who made the decision?" I asked. "We decided it here. Ilyich believed that we shouldn't leave the Whites a live banner to rally around, especially under the present difficult circumstances . . ." I did not ask any further questions, and considered the matter closed. Actually, the decision was not only expedient but necessary. The severity of this summary justice showed the world that we would continue to fight on mercilessly, stopping at nothing. The execution of the Tsar's family was needed not only in order to frighten, horrify, and dishearten the enemy, but also in order to shake up our own ranks, to show them that there was no turning back, that ahead lay either complete victory or complete ruin. In the intellectual circles of the Party there probably were misgivings and shakings of heads. But the masses of workers and soldiers had not a minute's doubt. They would not have understood and would not have accepted any other decision. *This* Lenin sensed well. The ability to think and feel for and with the masses was characteristic of him to the highest degree, especially at the great political turning points . . .

When I was abroad I read in *Poslednie Novosti* a description of the shooting, the burning of the bodies, etc. How much of all this is true and how much is invented, I have not the least idea, since I was never curious about *how* the sentence was carried out and, frankly, do not understand such curiosity.

* * *

The Socialist and the Communist parties of France are continuing their fatal work: they carry their opposition to a point quite sufficient to embitter the bourgeoisie and to bring about a mobilization of forces of reaction and additional arming of fascist detachments; but it is altogether insufficient for a revolutionary rallying of the proletariat. They provoke the class enemy as if on purpose and without giving anything to their own class. This is the shortest and most certain road to destruction.

April 10

Today, during a walk in the hills with N. — it was almost a summer day — I was thinking over my conversation with Lenin about a trial for the Tsar. It is possible that besides the time factor (we would "not have time" to bring a big trial to its conclusion, since the decisive events on the front might intervene), Lenin had another consideration with regard to the Tsar's family. Under judicial procedures, of course, execution of the family would have been impossible. The Tsar's family fell victim to that principle which constitutes the axis of monarchy: dynastic succession.

* * *

No news about Seryozha, and perhaps there won't be any for a long time. Long waiting has blunted the anxiety of the first days.

* * *

When I was getting ready to go to the front for the first time, between the fall of Simbirsk and that of Kazan, Lenin was in a gloomy mood. "Russians are too kind," "Russians are lazybones, softies," "It's a bowl of mush we have, and not a dictatorship . . ." I told him: "As the foundation for our military units we should use hard revolutionary nuclei, which will support iron discipline from *within;* create reliable security detachments which will act from *outside* in concert with the inner revolutionary nucleus of the detachment, and will not hesitate to shoot deserters; we should guarantee competent leadership by putting a commissar with a revolver over every *spets* [tsarist officer serving as technical expert in the Red Army]; we should set up military-revolutionary tribunals and establish decorations for individual bravery in battle." Lenin answered something like this: "That is all true, absolutely true, but there is not enough time; if we act drastically (which is absolutely necessary) our own party will interfere: they will whine, set every telephone ringing, tug at our coat-tails — in short, interfere. Of course, revolution hardens one, but there is too little time . . ." When Lenin became convinced by our talks that I believed in our success, he supported my trip wholeheartedly, helped with the arrangements, showed great concern, kept asking about ten times a day over the telephone how the preparations were going, whether we should not take an airplane along on the train, etc. . . .

Kazan fell. Lenin was wounded by the Social Revolutionist Kaplan. We recaptured Kazan. Simbirsk was retaken too. When I made a quick visit to Moscow, Lenin was convalescing in Gorki. Sverdlov told me: "Ilyich would like you to visit him. Shall we go together?" So we went. The manner in which Marya Ilyinishna and Nad[ezhda] Konst[antinovna] met me made me realize how impatiently and warmly they were expecting me. Lenin was in a fine humor and looked well physically. It seemed to me that he was looking at me with somehow different eyes. He had a way of *falling in love* with people when they showed him a certain side of themselves. There was a touch of this being "in love" in his excited attention. He listened eagerly to my stories about the front, and kept sighing with satisfaction, almost blissfully. "The game is won," he said, changing suddenly to a firm and serious tone. "If we have succeeded in establishing order in the army, it means we will establish it everywhere else. And the revolution — with order — will be unconquerable."

When Sverdlov and I were getting into our automobile, Lenin and N. K. stood on the balcony directly above the entrance, and again I felt the same slightly bashful, all-enveloping glance of Ilyich. He looked as if he wanted to say something more but could not find words. At that moment one of his bodyguards brought out some flowers in pots and started putting them into the car. Lenin's face darkened with anxiety. "You won't be uncomfortable?" he asked. I had paid no attention to the flowers and did not understand the reason for his concern. Only as we were approaching Moscow — the hungry, dirty Moscow of the fall months of 1918 — did I feel acutely ill at ease; was it appropriate to ride about with flowers at such a time? And just then I understood Lenin's concern: he had anticipated my uneasiness. He did have foresight.

At our next encounter I said to him: "The other day you asked about the flowers; I didn't even grasp, in the excitement of our meeting, what sort of 'discomfort' you had in mind. It suddenly dawned on me only as we were entering the city." "It made you look like a *meshochnik* [illegal trader]?" Ilyich asked quickly, and laughed gently. Again I caught that special friendly glance of his, which seemed to reflect his pleasure that I had understood him . . . How deeply, how distinctly, and how indelibly all the details, large and small, of the Gorki visit are engraved on my memory!

Lenin and I had several sharp clashes because, when I disagreed with him on serious questions, I always fought an all-out battle. Such cases, naturally, were memorable for everyone, and later on much was said and written about them by the epigones. But the instances when Lenin and I understood each other at a glance were a hundred times more numerous, and our solidarity always guaranteed the passage of a question in the Politburo without disputes. This solidarity meant a great deal to Lenin.

April 11

Baldwin thinks that Europe is a lunatic asylum; England is the only country that has kept her reason: she still has the King, the Commons, the Lords; England has avoided revolution, tyranny, and persecution (see his speech in Llandrindod).

As a matter of fact, Baldwin understands exactly nothing about what is taking place before his very eyes. There is a much greater distance between Baldwin and Lenin, as intellectual types, than between the Celtic druids and Baldwin. England is nothing but the last ward of the European madhouse, and quite possibly it will prove to be the ward for particularly violent cases.

Before the last Labourite government, just at the time of the election, the Webbs, Sidney and Beatrice, came to visit us at Prinkipo. These "socialists" were quite willing to accept Stalin's socialism in one country for Russia. They expected, not without gloating, a cruel civil war in the U. S. But for England (and Scandinavia) they reserved the privilege of peaceful evolutionary socialism. In order to account for unpleasant facts — such as the October Revolution, outbursts of the class struggle, and fascism — and at the same time preserve their Fabian prejudices and predilections, the Webbs — to suit their Anglo-Saxon empiricism — had created a theory of "types" of social development and made a bargain with history to obtain a peaceful type for England. In fact, at that time Sidney Webb was about to receive from his King the title of Lord Passfield, so that he might peacefully reconstruct society as His Majesty's minister.*

Of course, the Webbs are closer to Baldwin than to Lenin. I listened to the Webbs as if they were emanations from the next world, although they are very educated people. It's true that they boasted of not belonging to any church.

* An amusing touch: Sidney Webb informed me, with particular emphasis, that he was able to leave England for a few weeks only because he was not standing for Parliament. He obviously expected me to ask, "*Why?*" in order to inform me about his pending elevation to the peerage. I saw in his eyes that he was expecting a question, but refrained from asking anything in order to avoid causing any embarrassment. The question of the peerage never even occurred to me; rather I thought that Webb, in his old age, had renounced active political life, and naturally I did not want to pursue that subject. Only later, when the new ministry was formed, I understood what had been going on: the author of research reports on industrial democracy was proudly looking forward to bearing the title of lord!

April 14

In Stresa, three socialist turncoats, Mussolini, Laval, and MacDonald, represent the "national" interests of their countries. The most contemptible and incompetent is MacDonald. There is something of the flunkey running all through him, even in his posture when talking to Mussolini (see the newspaper picture). It is so characteristic of this man that during his first ministry he hastened to grant a position to Mosley, the aristocratic coxcomb who had only recently joined the Labour Party as a shortcut to a career. And now that same Mosley is trying to change sane old England into merely another ward of the European lunatic asylum. And if he does not succeed in this, somebody else certainly will — the minute fascism is victorious in France. This time the possible advent to power of the Labourites will give a great stimulus to the development of British fascism and in general will open up a stormy chapter in the history of England, contrary to all the historical and philosophic conceptions of the Baldwins and the Webbs.

In September 1930, about two or three months after the Webbs, Cynthia Mosley, the wife of the adventurer and daughter of the notorious Lord Curzon, visited me at Prinkipo. At that stage her husband was still attacking MacDonald "from the left." After some hesitation I agreed to a meeting which, however, proved banal in the extreme. The "Lady" arrived with a female traveling companion, referred contemptuously to MacDonald, and spoke of her sympathies toward Soviet Russia. But the enclosed letter from her is an adequate specimen of her attitude at that time. About three years later the young woman suddenly died. I don't know if she lived long enough to cross over to the fascist camp.

About that time or a little later I received a letter from Beatrice Webb in which — on her own initiative — she tried to justify or explain the refusal of the Labour Government to grant me a visa. (This letter ought to be looked up, but I am without a secretary now.) I did not answer her: there was no point . . .

[*Letter, typewritten in English, pasted in.*]

COPY:

M. TOKATLIYAN OTELI
Beyoglu Istiklal Caddesi
Hotel M. Tokatlian
Pera, Rue Istiklal

Istanbul, September 4,
[*in ink:*] 1930

Dear Comrade Trotsky.

I would like above all things to see you for a few moments. There is no good reason why you should see me as 1) I belong to the Labour Party in England who were so ridiculous and refused to allow you in, but also I belong to the I.L.P. and we did try our very best to make them change their minds, and 2) I am daughter of Lord Curzon who was Minister for Foreign Affairs in London when you were in Russia!

On the other hand I am an ardent Socialist. I am a member of the House of Commons. I think less than nothing of the present Government. I have just finished reading your life which inspired me as no other book has done for ages. I am a great admirer of yours. These days when great men seem so very few and far between it would be a great privilege to meet one of the enduring figures of our age and I do hope with all my heart you will grant me that privilege. I need hardly say I came as a private person, not a journalist or *anything* but myself — I am on my way to Russia, I leave for Batoum — Tiflis — Rostov — Kharkov and Moscow by boat Monday. I have come to Prinkipo this afternoon especially to try to see you, but if it were not convenient I could come out again anyday till Monday. I do hope however you could allow me a few moments *this* afternoon.

Yours fraternally
CYNTHIA MOSLEY

April 27

Again a long interruption. I have been preoccupied with the affairs of the Fourth International, in particular the programmatic documents of the South African section. Fires of revolutionary Marxist thought have been kindled everywhere. Our groups are studying, criticizing, learning, and thinking — this is their great advantage over both the socialists and the communists. This advantage will tell in great events.

Yesterday N. and I were walking in a drizzling rain. We caught up with the following group: a young woman with a year-old baby in her arms, in front of her a little girl of two or three; the woman was in the very last stages of pregnancy; in her hand she held a rope to which a goat was tied, and the goat had a kid with it. In this manner the five of them — or rather the six — were slowly going up the road. All the time the goat kept trying to get off the road to savor the green leaves of the bushes; the woman would tug at the rope; in the meantime the little girl would lag behind or run ahead; the kid would get tangled up in the bushes . . . On the way back we met the same family group again — they were slowly continuing their advance toward the village. In the still fresh face of the woman there was submission and patience. She was probably Spanish or

Italian, perhaps even Polish — there are quite a few foreign working-class families here.

Still no news about Seryozha's fate.

Le Temps in a report from Moscow notes that this year's May Day slogans spoke only of the struggle against the Trotskyists and the Zinovievists and did not mention the right opposition at all. This time the turn to the right will go farther than ever before, much farther than Stalin foresees.

On the cover of the latest (43rd) number of the *Bulletin* of the Russian Opposition, edited by me, I noticed — not without surprise — the inscription: *Seventh year of publication.* This means: the seventh year of my third emigration. The first emigration lasted two and a half years (1902–1905); the second, ten years (1907–1917); the third . . . How long will the third one last?

During the first and the second emigrations, until the beginning of the war, I traveled freely all over Europe and gave talks, unhindered, on the approach of social revolution. Only in Prussia were precautionary measures necessary; in the rest of Germany benevolence reigned on the part of the police. This was even more the case in the other countries of Europe, including the Balkans. I traveled with some sort of doubtful Bulgarian passport which, I think, I was asked to show only one single time, on the Prussian border. Those were blissful times! In Paris, in open political meetings, the different factions of the Russian emigration fought until midnight and after over the problem of terror and armed uprising . . . Policemen stood in the street (Avenue Choisy, 110, I believe), but never entered the hall and never checked upon those who did. Only after midnight the owner of the café sometimes turned off the electric lights in order to quiet the mounting passions — there was no other control over the destructive activity of the emigration. How much stronger and more secure the capitalist system felt in those years!

April 29

The day before yesterday Edouard Herriot said in Lyon:

> Notre Révolution, nous l'avons faite. Nous avons même attendu plus d'un demi-siècle pour en recueillir les bienfaits. Nous possédons aujourd'hui les cadres nécessaires pour toutes les réformes possibles, pour toutes les évolutions, pour tous les progrès.
> [*Clipping pasted in. The first two sentences underlined in ink, and the whole put in quotation marks in ink.*]

That is why Herriot refuses to enter into agreement with those who advocate "revolutionary action."

> Nous ne saurions donc nous accorder ni avec ceux qui se réclament de l'action révolutionnaire, ni avec ceux qui nient la nécessité d'organiser, selon ses besoins, la défense nationale.
> [*Clipping pasted in. The whole is enclosed by parentheses in ink.*]

A great historical epoch speaks through the mouth of Herriot — the epoch of conservative democracy, the epoch of highest prosperity for the average Frenchman. As always, a completed epoch defines itself with the greatest clarity just before its collapse.

"We have made our revolution," says the bourgeoisie (of

yesteryear) through the mouth of Herriot. "But we have not yet made *ours*," replies the proletariat. Precisely because of this, today's bourgeoisie is unwilling to tolerate *"les cadres nécessaires pour toutes les réformes" — cadres* created by the revolution. Herriot is yesterday. The very latest issue of *Le Temps* (April 28) prints an unusually Jesuitical editorial on the subject of the fascist leagues. The young people are "carried away"? *"Il faut l'aimer puisqu'elle est l'avenir."* The big bourgeoisie has already made its decision.

* * *

Judging by the latest reports, the congress of the Comintern will apparently still take place in Moscow in May. Evidently Stalin simply could not cancel or postpone the congress any longer; it would have been too much of a scandal. It is also possible that the futility of Eden's visit and the difficulties encountered in the negotiations with France prompted the idea of "scaring" their "associates" with this congress. Alas, this congress will not frighten any one!

* * *

LE PAPE BÉNIT PAR T. S. F. LES FIDÉLES DE LOURDES

Lourdes, 28 avril. — La messe pontificale a pris fin aujourd'hui vers 16 heures 20.

Un peu après, les haut-parleurs ont annoncé qu'ils allaient faire entendre la Cité du Vatican et que Sa Sainteté Pie XI allait donner sa bénédiction aux fidèles. En effet, quelques minutes après, au milieu du plus profond silence, Pie XI addressa à la foule tous ses remerciements, toute sa reconnaissance d'être venue si nombreuse de toutes les parties du monde.

[*Clipping pasted in. The word* "Lourdes" *is underlined in ink.*]

Last year N. and I were in Lourdes. What crudeness, insolence, nastiness! A shop for miracles, a business office for trafficking in grace. The Grotto itself makes a miserable impression. That, of course, is a psychological calculation of the clerics: not to frighten the little people away by the grandeur of their commercial enterprise; little people are afraid of shop-windows which are too resplendent. At the same time they are the most faithful and profitable customers. But best of all is the papal blessing broadcast to Lourdes by — radio. The paltry miracles of the Gospels side by side with the radiotelephone! And what could be more absurd and disgusting than the union of proud technology with the sorcery of the Roman chief druid? Indeed, the thinking of mankind is bogged down in its own excrement.

May 1935

May 2

The Radicals have broken up the election bloc in almost the entire country. Now the Socialists (including the local municipal clique of Dr. Martin) are accused by their erstwhile allies of "destructive" and "antinational" tendencies. In vain will Martin swear to his patriotism and love of order. Nothing will help him! Instead of breaking with the Radicals and issuing their own indictment of radicalism, the "socialists" have found themselves ejected from the joint election bloc and accused of national treason.

The Radicals found the necessary "courage" in the depth of their cowardice: they act under the whip of big capital — which will betray them to fascism tomorrow. The Socialists could not manifest any semblance of initiative except beneath the whip of the Communists. But the Stalinists themselves are in need of a whip. To tell the truth, it is too late for any whip to help them. What will soon be needed is a broom — to sweep out all the refuse of what was intended to become a revolutionary party.

May 4

The Franco-Soviet agreement has been signed. All the comments of the French press, despite differences in shading, are agreed on one point: the significance of the treaty is that it ties down the U.S.S.R. and prevents it from flirting with Germany; our *real* "friends," as before, are Italy and England plus the Little Entente and Poland. The U.S.S.R.

is looked upon as a hostage rather than as an ally. *Le Temps* gives an exciting picture of the Moscow military parade on May Day, but adds significantly: the real strength of an army is to be judged not by parades but by industrial power, with the coefficients of transport, supply, etc.

Potemkin exchanged telegrams with Herriot, calling him "the friend of my country." At the beginning of the Civil War Potemkin found himself at the front, probably in one of the countless mobilizations. Stalin was in charge of the southern front at that time, and he appointed Potemkin as the chief of the Political Department in one of the armies (or divisions?). During one of my tours I visited that political department. Potemkin, whom I then saw for the first time, greeted me with an unusually obsequious and false speech. The Bolshevik workers and commissars were obviously embarrassed. I almost pushed Potemkin away from the table and, without replying to his greeting, began talking about the situation on the front . . . Some time later the Politburo, with Stalin's participation, was checking over the staff of workers on the southern front. Potemkin's name came up. "An unbearable character," I said, "not at all one of us." Stalin stood up for him: "He put the fear of God into some division on the southern front," meaning that he disciplined them. Zinoviev, who had known Potemkin a little in Petersburg, supported me. "Potemkin," he said, "is like Professor Reisner, only worse." I learned then for the first time, I believe, that Potemkin too was a former professor. "But in what way is he really so bad?" Lenin asked. "He is a courtier!" I answered. Lenin evidently understood that as an allusion to Potemkin's servile attitude toward Stalin. But that did not even enter my head. I was merely thinking of the indecent welcoming speech Potemkin had addressed to me. I don't remember whether I ever cleared up the misunderstanding.

May Day in France passed by in an atmosphere of humiliation and weakness. The Minister of the Interior had prohibited demonstrations, even in the Bois de Vincennes; and indeed, despite all the bragging and threats of *L'Humanité,* there were no demonstrations at all. May Day is only a continuation and further manifestation of the entire course of the struggle. If in March and April the leading organizations do nothing but hold back, restrain, confuse and demoralize the workers, then naturally no miracle will produce an outburst of aggressive firmness on a certain day on the calendar, the first of May. Léon Blum and Marcel Cachin as of old are systematically paving the way for fascism.

* * *

Life goes on, as before, in a modified prison style: between four walls, without people. Once a day a walk along a path, with back yards and gardens on one side, and the ascent into the mountains on the other. The path leads to villages at either end, so that the walk is a short one, about 30 minutes long; to stretch it out to an hour you have to walk there and back twice. That too resembles prison walks . . . One could, of course, walk up the mountain — sometimes we do — but this is fatiguing and hard on the heart. Once a week or once a fortnight, N. goes shopping in Grenoble, but I hardly ever get out . . . But all this is trivial detail compared with the realization that the fascist reaction is moving closer every day.

* * *

Tomorrow is the municipal election, which will have an important symptomatic meaning. The Radicals have split. The left minority is for the cartel. The right majority is for a national bloc. This split is a very significant stage in the decline of radicalism. But this stage may take the paradoxical form of an increase in votes in the towns: the entire bourgeois and the petty bourgeois reaction will vote for the Radicals. But the Radicals will not escape their destiny.

April [sic] *5*

Election today. A mobilization of all the forces of law and order is taking place under the slogan of "anticollectivism." In the meanwhile neither working-class party has dared to unfold the socialist banner, for fear of scaring away the "middle classes." Thus these ill-fated parties derive nothing but losses from their socialist program.

* * *

The radio is playing *Madame Butterfly*. It is Sunday; we are all alone in the house: our landlords have either gone to visit someone or to perform their civic duty — to vote . . . A group of cyclists passed by in the street; someone at the head was singing the "International" — apparently a workers' election picket. The two working-class parties and the two trade union organizations, which are completely discredited politically, still possess the tremendous force of historical inertia. The organic character of social processes, including political ones, is revealed with a special immediacy during critical epochs, when the old "revolutionary" organizations are shown to possess hindquarters of lead, which prevent them from performing the necessary about-face at the right moment. How absurd are the "theories" of M[ax] Eastman and others about revolutionaries as "engineers" who — presumably according to their own blueprints — build new social forms out of the materials at hand. And this American mechanistic theory tries to pass itself off as an advance over dialectical materialism! The social processes, in the broad sense, are much closer to organic than to mechanical ones. A revolutionary who relies on the scientific theory of social development is much closer in his mode of thinking and working to the doctor, and the surgeon in particular, than to the engineer — although even about bridge-building the American Eastman has truly childish notions. Like the doctor, the revolutionary Marxist has to rely on the autonomous rhythm of the vital processes . . . Under present conditions in France the Marxist appears to be a "sectarian"; the inertia of history, including the inertia of the working-class organizations, is against him . . . The correctness of the Marxist prognosis is *bound* to reveal itself, but it may do so in two ways: either the masses will take the path of Marxist politics before it is too late, or the proletariat will be smashed. Such is the alternative of the *present* epoch.

In 1926 N. and I were in Berlin at this time of year. Weimar democracy was still in full flower. The policies of the German Communist Party had long since left the Marxist rails — if it can be said that they had ever been fully on them — but the party itself still represented an impressive force. Incognito, we attended the May Day demonstrations on the Alexanderplatz. An enormous mass of people, a multitude of banners, confident speeches. My feeling was: it will be hard to maneuver that unwieldy bulk . . .

All the more disheartening was the impression made on

me by the Politburo meeting on the first Thursday after my return to Moscow. Molotov was then in charge of the Comintern. He is a man who is not stupid and he has some strength of character, but he is limited and obtuse and lacks imagination. He is not familiar with Europe and does not read foreign languages. Sensing his own weakness, he was all the more stubborn in maintaining his "independence." The others simply supported him. I remember Rudzutak arguing with me and trying to correct a translation of mine from *L'Humanité,* calling it "tendentious." He took the newspaper away from me and, running his fingers along the lines, kept losing the place and getting mixed up, covering himself with insolence as with a shield. Once again, the others "supported" him. A system of mutual guarantee had been established as an inviolable law. (By a special secret decision of 1924 the members of the Politburo undertook never to debate openly with one another and invariably to support one another in polemics with me.) I stood before these people as if I were standing before a blank wall. But that, of course, was not the main thing. Behind the ignorance, the narrowness, the obstinacy and hostility of separate individuals, one could almost feel with one's fingers the social features of a privileged caste, very sensitive, very perceptive, very enterprising in everything that concerned *its own interests.* And it was upon this caste that the German Communist Party was entirely dependent. That was the historical tragedy of the situation. The dénouement came in 1933 when the huge Communist Party of Germany, undermined from within by lies and falsities, crumbled to dust at the advent of fascism. This Molotov and Rudzutak did not foresee. But it could have been foreseen . . .

That the trouble did not stem merely from individual

limitations or the personal myopia of Molotov is proved by the whole further course of events. The bureaucracy has remained true to itself. Its basic features have become still more deeply fixed. In France the Comintern is conducting a policy no less ruinous than its German policy. Meanwhile, historical inertia is still operative. Those youths on bicycles singing the "International" are almost certainly followers of the Comintern, which cannot bring them anything but defeat and humiliation. In general it is impossible for people to come out of the woods on to the main road of history without the conscious participation of the "sectarians," i.e., the Marxist minority, which today is pushed aside. But it must be a question of participation in an *organic* process. One must know its laws, as a doctor must know the "healing power of nature."

* * *

I have been unwell, after two weeks of intensive work, and have read several novels. *Clarisse et sa fille* by Marcel Prévost. The novel is highly virtuous, but it is the virtue of an old cocotte. Prévost as a psychoanalyst! He refers to himself as a "psychologist" more than once. He also cites Paul Bourget as an authority on affairs of the heart. I remember with what well-deserved contempt, even disgust, Octave Mirbeau spoke about Bourget. And really, what superficial, false, and rotten literature this is!

A Russian story: *Kolkhida* by Paustovsky. The author is evidently a sailor of the old school who took part in the Civil War. A gifted man, technically superior to the so-called "proletarian writers." He paints nature well; you can discern the sharp eye of a seaman. At times, in his descriptions of Soviet life (in the Transcaucasus) he reminds one of a good gymnast with his elbows tied. But there are some stirring pictures of work, sacrifice and enthusiasm. Strange as it may seem, his most successful character is an *English* sailor who finds himself stranded in the Caucasus and is drawn into working for the cause.

The third novel — *The Great Assembly-line,* by Yakov Ilyin. This one is a pure specimen of what is called "proletarian literature," and not the worst specimen at that. The author depicts the "romance" of a tractor factory — how it is constructed and put in operation. There are a great many technical problems and details, and still more discussions about them. It is written in a comparatively lively style but it is still rather the style of a literary apprentice. In this "proletarian" work the proletariat is put *far* into the background. The foreground is taken up by the organizers, administrators, technicians, managers and — machine tools. The gulf between the upper stratum and the mass runs through the whole epic of this American assembly-line on the Volga.

The author is extremely pious about the party line; his attitude toward the leaders is permeated with official veneration. It is difficult to define either the degree of sincerity of those feelings, since they are coerced and obligatory for all, or the degree of hostility toward the Opposition. The Trotskyists do occupy a definite, although secondary, place in the novel; and the author diligently ascribes to them views borrowed from the denunciatory editorials of *Pravda.* And still, in spite of its strictly good intentions, at times the novel reads like a satire on Stalin's regime. The enormous factory is put into operation before it is finished: there are machines, but no place for the workers to live. The work is not organized; there is not enough water; anarchy reigns everywhere. It is necessary to close down the factory temporarily to make further preparations. Close down the factory? But what will Stalin say? But this was promised to the Party Congress, etc. Disgusting Byzantinism instead of businesslike considerations. The result is a monstrous squandering of manpower and — bad tractors. The author quotes Stalin's speech at the meeting of industrial administrators: "To slow down the tempos? Impossible. What about the West?" (In April, 1927, Stalin had argued that the problem of the rate of industrialization had no relation to the problem of building socialism within a capitalist encirclement: "tempo" is our "internal affair.") Consequently it is "impossible" to reduce the tempos ordered from higher up. But why is the rate of expansion given as 25, and not 40 or 75? The ordered coefficient of expansion is never reached anyway, and the price for approaching it is low quality and wearing down of workers' lives and machinery. You can see it all in Ilyin's novel, in spite of the official piety of the author . . .

Some of the details are striking. Ordzhonikidze (in the novel) says "thou" to a worker, while the latter answers him with "you." The whole dialogue is carried on in this style, which the author himself regards as the natural order of things.

But the grimmest aspect of the assembly-line romance is the absence of political rights and the lack of individuality on the part of the workers, especially the proletarian youth, who are taught only to obey. A young engineer who rebels against the excessive assignments is reminded by the Party Committee of his recent "Trotskyism" and threatened with expulsion. Young party members argue about why nobody in the younger generation has done anything outstanding in any field. The disputants console themselves with rather confused arguments. "Couldn't it be because we are smothered?" — one of them lets slip this remark. He is attacked by all: we don't need freedom of discussion, we have the guidance of the party and "Stalin's instructions." The guidance of the party — without discussion — this is just what "Stalin's instructions" are, and they in their turn merely constitute an empirical summing up of the experience of the bureaucracy. The dogma of bureaucratic infallibility suffocates the young people by infusing their characters with servility, Byzantinism, and false "wisdom." There probably are mature people working in hiding somewhere. But on those who give the official coloring to the younger generation there is the indelible imprint of immaturity.

[*End of Notebook 1*]

1935

May 8

Word from Moscow via Paris: "Of course you must have had letters concerning their little unpleasantness." This obviously refers to Seryozha (and his companion). But there have been no letters; or rather the letter must have perished in transit, like most of our letters, even quite innocent ones. What does a "little" unpleasantness mean? On what scale is it "little"? No news from Seryozha himself . . .

Old age is the most unexpected of all the things that happen to a man.

The Norwegian Labor Government seems to have given a firm promise to grant me a visa. It looks as if we should have to take advantage of it. To stay longer in France would involve greater and greater difficulties, in either of the two alternatives: in case there is an uninterrupted advance of reaction or in case there is a successful development of the revolutionary movement.

Being unable to deport me to another country, the government which theoretically "deported" me from France does not dare to send me to one of the colonies, because that would raise too big a stir and would create a pretext for constant agitation. But as the domestic situation grows tenser, these secondary considerations will lose their importance — and N. and I may find ourselves in one of the colonies. Not in the comparatively favorable conditions of North Africa, of course, but somewhere very remote . . . That would mean political isolation, immeasurably more complete than Prinkipo. Under these circumstances it is wiser to leave France while there is time.

It is true that the municipal elections provide evidence of a certain "stabilization" of the political situation. This fact is stressed by the whole press in every possible key, albeit with different interpretations. Nevertheless, it would be the greatest foolishness to believe in this "stability." The majority vote as they did "last time," merely because you have to vote some way. Not one of the classes has as yet definitely accepted the new orientation. But all objective conditions are compelling them to accept it; and the staffs for it have already been formed, at least by the bourgeoisie. The "interruption of gradualness" in this process can come about very fast, and in any case will occur very abruptly.

Norway is not France, of course: an unfamiliar language,

a small country, off the main track, delayed mail, etc. But still it is much better than Madagascar. The language I could manage quickly — enough to understand the newspapers. The record of the Norwegian Labor Party is very interesting, both in itself and especially on the eve of the accession to power of the Labour Party [*in English*] in Great Britain. Of course, in the event of the victory of fascism in France, the Scandinavian "last ditch" of democracy would not hold out long. But anyway, in the present situation we can in general only hope for a "breathing spell."

In the last letter N. received from him Seryozha wrote, as if by the way: "The general situation is proving extremely difficult, much more difficult than you can imagine . . ." At first these words might have seemed to have a purely personal character. But by now it has become completely clear that Seryozha is speaking of the political situation — as it has shaped itself for him since the murder of Kirov and the new wave of persecution connected with it. (The letter is dated December 9, 1934). Truly, it is not hard to imagine what he must be experiencing — not only at meetings and in reading the papers, but also in personal encounters, conversations and (undoubtedly) countless provocations on the part of petty careerists and scoundrels. If Seryozha had an active interest in politics and a partisan spirit, all these painful experiences would be justified. But he completely lacks that inner resource. It is therefore that much harder for him . . .

I have taken up the diary again because I cannot undertake anything else; the ebb and flow of my capacity for work have become very marked . . .

Last summer, when we were wandering about after being driven out of Barbizon, N. and I had to separate: she remained in Paris, while I, with two young comrades, kept moving from hotel to hotel. An agent of the *Sûreté générale* followed close on our heels. We stopped at Chamonix. Apparently the police suspected that I had some intentions concerning Switzerland or Italy, and gave me away to the newspapermen. Early in the morning, in a barber shop, M. read in a local newspaper a sensational notice about our whereabouts. N. had just arrived from Paris to join me. We managed to disappear before the notice could create the necessary effect. We had a small, rather antique Ford: its description and registration number appeared in print. We had to get rid of that car and buy another, also a Ford, but a still older model. Only after this incident did the *Sûreté* think of informing us that it was not advisable for me to stay in Departments situated along the border. We decided to rent a summer place in some spot away from the frontier. But we had to spend two or three weeks looking for one: it had to be no closer than 300 kilometers to Paris, not closer than 30 kilometers to the center of a Department, not in an industrial district, etc. — such were the conditions laid down by the police. We decided to put up in a *pension* while the search went on. But this did not prove to be so simple: we could not register with our own documents, and the police would not allow us to register with false ones. Actually, French citizens are not required to show their documents; but in a *pension* with a *table d'hôte* we would have had some trouble passing for French. And so, for such an insignificant business as settling for two weeks in a modest suburban *pension*, under the observation of an agent of the *Sûreté nationale*, we had to undertake a very complex operation. We decided to be French citizens of foreign extraction. To this end we enlisted the services of a young French comrade with a Dutch name to play the part of our nephew. How to get rid of the *table d'hôte*? I proposed that we should don mourning and give this as an excuse for eating in our own room. The "nephew" was to eat at the common table and observe the goings-on in the house.

The plan encountered, first of all, resistance from N.: to put on mourning and engage in dissimulation — she regarded this as something offensive to her very self. But the advantages of the plan were too obvious, and she had to give in. Our arrival at the *pension* could not have gone better. Even the three South American students living there — a breed little inclined to discipline — stopped talking and bowed respectfully to people in mourning. I was only a little surprised at the engravings hanging in the hall: "The King's Cavalryman," "The Parting of Marie-Antoinette with Her Children," and the like.

The riddle was quickly solved. After dinner our "nephew" came to us very much disturbed: we had landed in a royalist pension! *L'Action française* was the only newspaper recognized in the house. The recent bloody events in the town (an antifascist demonstration) had inflamed political passions in the *pension*. In the center of a royalist "conspiracy" stood the landlady, a nurse who had been awarded a medal for service in the imperialist war; she maintained close personal connections with the royalist and fascist circles in the town.

Next day, by established custom, G., an agent of the *Sûreté* and professional defender of the Republic, moved into the *pension.* As it happened, during those very weeks Léon Daudet had been conducting in *L'Action française* a wild campaign against the *Sûreté* as a gang of swindlers, traitors, and murderers. Daudet in particular accused the *Sûreté* of killing his son Philippe. The agent of the *Sûreté,* a man about forty-five years old, proved to be a most worldly gentleman: he had been everywhere, knew everything, and could with equal ease converse about the makes of automobiles, the vintages of wines, the comparative armaments of the different countries, the latest criminal trials and the most recent works of literature. In questions of politics he strove to maintain a tactful neutrality. But the *pension*-keeper (or more correctly, the *pension*-keeper's husband, a traveling salesman) invariably appealed to him for sympathy in his royalist views. "Anyhow, *L'Action française* is the best French newspaper!" G. would answer pacifyingly, "Charles Maurras really deserves respect, that cannot be denied, but Daudet is inexcusably rude." The *pension*-keeper insisted politely: "Of course, Daudet is rather rude at times, but he has a right to be; why, those villains have killed his son!"

One must add that G. participated very directly in the "affair" of young Philippe Daudet, so that the accusation was directed against him personally. But G. did not lose his dignity even then. "With this I do not agree," he replied to the unsuspecting landlord. "We will agree to differ." After each *repas* our "nephew" would tell us about these Molière-like scenes; and half-an-hour of merry, though suppressed, laughter (we were of course in mourning) repaid us at least partially for the discomforts of our existence. On Sunday N. and I went out "to Mass" — really for a walk. This heightened our prestige in the house.

Just at the time of our stay in the *pension* the weekly *L'Illustration* printed a large photograph of both N. and me. I was not easily recognizable with my moustache and beard shaved off and my haircut changed, but N.'s likeness was very good . . . As I remember, there was even some talk about us at the table in connection with this photograph. The first to sound the alarm was G. "You should leave immediately!" He was apparently altogether bored in the modest *pension*. But we were firm, and remained beneath the royalist roof until we had rented a summer house.

Here again we had a piece of bad luck. The prefect of the Department (through our French comrade M., who conducted the negotiations with him) allowed us to settle anywhere at a distance of thirty kilometers from town. But when M. informed the Prefect of our address, after the house had already been rented, the latter exclaimed: "You have chosen the most inappropriate place! That is a hotbed of clericalism. The *maire* is a personal enemy of mine!" And indeed, in all the rooms of our cottage (a modest village house) there were crucifixes and pious engravings. The Prefect insisted that we change our quarters. But we had already concluded an agreement with the landlady; and the traveling and moving had bankrupted us as it was. We refused to leave the house. About two weeks later the local blackmailing weekly printed a report that T. with his wife and secretaries had settled in such and such a place. The address was not given, but the region was indicated quite precisely within several square kilometers. There could not be any doubt that it was a maneuver on the part of the Prefect, and that his next action would be to impose upon us an exact address. We had to leave the cottage in a hurry . . .

The jubilee celebrations in England made a degrading impression: a gaudy exhibition of servility and stupidity. The big bourgeoisie at least knows what it is doing: this medieval lumber will come in very handy in forthcoming battles as a first barricade against the proletariat.

May 9

An issue of the German newspaper *Unser Wort* is due to come out in just a few days, with an article of mine, in which I speak very sharply about the Norwegian Labor Party and its policies while in power (concerning in particular the question of the voting of the household budget for the king). There would be nothing surprising if this article should induce the Norwegian government to refuse me a visa at the very last moment. That would be very annoying, but . . . to be expected.

May 10

The Bureau of the Second International has passed a resolution on the danger of war. The source of the danger is *Hitler*; salvation lies in the *League of Nations*; the most reliable means is *disarmament*; the "democratic" governments cooperating with the *U.S.S.R.* are solemnly hailed. If the phraseology were changed just a little bit, this document could be signed by the Presidium of the Third International as well. In essence, the resolution is immeasurably worse than the manifesto of the Basel Congress (1912) on the eve of the war . . .*

No, there is no room for our epoch in these narrow, conservative, cowardly brains. Nothing will save the profiteers of the labor movement today. They will be crushed. In the blood of wars and revolts a new generation will rise, worthy of the epoch and its tasks.

May 13

Pilsudski is dead . . . I never met him personally. But even at the time of my first exile in Siberia (1900–1902), I heard ardent tributes to him from exiled Poles. At that time Pilsudski was one of the young leaders of the PPS (Polish Socialist Party), and consequently, in the broad sense of the word, a "comrade." Mussolini was a comrade too, as well as MacDonald and Laval . . . What a gallery of traitors!

I have received some confidential information about the last session of the Bureau of the Second International (See May 10). These people are inimitable. The letter deserves to be saved.

[*Enclosure: letter typewritten in French, the lines italicized below heavily underlined in pencil. Signed in ink. Misspellings preserved.*]

Bruxelles, 9 Mai 1935

Camarade L. D.

Voici quelques détails sur la réunion du B.E. de l'I.O.S.

1° Ci joint vous trouverez la résolution tel qu'elle est sortie de la Commission. J'y ai apporté les changements selon le texte paru dans les journaux.

* One must now expect Hitler to propose general disarmament and to make this demand a condition of the return of Germany to the League of Nations. This sort of competition with Litvinov is quite free of risk for German imperialism.

2° Van der Velde n'est plus membre du B.E. Les statuts ne lui permettent pas d'être ministre et en même temps membre du bureau. Mais il assiste a chaque réunion du secrétariat. Il a même proposé de se réunir dans son *cabinet ministériel. Adler s'y est opposé.*

3° Il assistait également à la première réunion du Bureau Exécutif. Les proces verbaux ne peuvent en faire motion.

4° Breitscheid est venu rendre visite à ses amis mais n'a pas assisté à la réunion.

5° La presse ne cite pas les noms des délégués autrichiens. Ce furent Bauer et Polak. De même pour celui de la Tchecoslovaqui; c'était Léo de Winter.

6° Pas un mot sur la III Internationale.

7° Toute la scession fut prise par l'élaboration de la résolution définitive dont cela de Blum était à l'origine.

8° On c'est occupé pendant cinq minutes à constituer une *commission qui fonctionnerait . . . . pendant la guerre. C'est Dan qui a fait* cette proposition. Après la réunion Blum est allé lui demander (en se moquant de lui) si c'était lui qui été l'auteur véritable de la proposition. Dan à répondu que c'était là une proposition des socialistes polonais.

9° Pendant deux jours on a discuté cette résolution. Celui qui ergotait le plus était le délégué anglais. Notre camarade a eu l'impression qu'il sentait (William Gillis; les autres se sont tu) toute la résponsabilité qu'il prenait pour le Labour Party. Les autres avait plutot l'air d'agir en leur nom propre.

10° Le délégue italien aussi était plus ou moins en opposition. Il aurait voullu absolument qu'on parle *dans la résolution du plan impérialiste du fascisme italien en Afrique.* C'est à la suite de son intervention que l'amendement souligné par moi dans le texte a été ajouté. Ceci sans doute pour qu'il puisse s'expliquer devant sa section. Les autres ne voullurent absolument pas que le nom de l'Abissinie figure dans le texte.

Notre camarade n'ayant pas pu assister à toutes les séances n'a pu avoir de meilieurs renseignements.

Salutations communistes.

G. Ver.

Especially good is the "commission in case of war" — what a heroic attempt to rise above one's own nature! These gentlemen don't want to be caught unawares by a war this time. And so they create . . . a secret commission. But where and how can they buy insurance that the members of the commission will not find themselves on opposite sides of the trenches, not only physically but also politically? To this question the wise men have no answer . . .

May 14

Pilsudski was called as a witness in the trial of Aleksandr Ulyanov, the older brother of Lenin. In the same trial (the attempt on Alexander III's life on March 1, 1887) the younger brother of Pilsudski was a defendant . . .

During the last few decades history has been working fast. And yet how endless some periods of reaction have seemed, especially 1907–1912 . . . In Prague a few days ago they celebrated the eightieth birthday of Lazarev, the old *Narodnik* . . . In Moscow Vera Figner is still alive, and many other old-timers. Of the people who made the first steps toward mass revolutionary work in tsarist Russia, not all have yet left the stage. And at the same time we face the problem of the bureaucratic degeneration of the workers' state . . . No, contemporary history is running in high gear. The only pity is that organism-destroying microbes work even faster. If they consume me before the world revolution takes a new big step forward — and it does look that way — I shall still pass into nonexistence with an indestructible confidence in the victory of the cause I have served all my life.

May 15

The *Sûreté* is obviously showing off its knowledge of the circumstances of my life. One of my friends, who acts as a constant mediator between me and the authorities, sent me the following excerpt from his dialogue with the Secretary General of the *Sûreté.*

[*Enclosure: letter in French, in longhand. The mistakes have been preserved.*]

Extraits d'un dialogue —

C Ne pensez-vous pas que le désir de se déplacer de T ne provienne pas de ses difficultés avec son logeur?

H Difficultés? Croyez-vous qu'il y ait des difficultés?

C Certainnement; oh le bonhomme ne doit pas être commode voyez-vous; il n'y a pas qu'avec nous que cela ne vas pas! (sourires . . .)

H Difficultés me semble un bien gros mot, j'ai peut être eu en effet l'impression de petits malentendus mais jamais je n'ai entendu parler de difficultés! Je pense que vos "informateurs" ont bien grossi les choses pour avoir le mérite d'un beau "rapport."—

C Détrompez-vous c'est un ami qui, par hasard, m'a appris la chose et pas du tout en mal, car il ne veut rien de mauvais à T et était, au contraire, très embêté de la situation créé . . .

H Je pense que vouz avez été trompé —

C Je ne pense pas du tout; nous préférions du reste qu'il n'en soit rien car nous serions assez embêtés si son logeur l'obligeait à partir, nous n'avons aucun intérêt à ce que cette histoire recommence!

H Je dois vous dire que j'ai fait une petite enquête sur le voyage, que vous m'avez signalé, de son fils dans l'Est — L'interressé m'a demontré qu'il n'avait pas du tout voyagé! — Vos agents ont du le confondre avec un quelconque ami de T.

C Je ne crois pas; nos informations sont excellentes.

H La police croit toujours ses informations excellentes mais elle reçoit trop souvent des informations interressés pour avoir le droit de les déclarer excellentes. Le jeune homme prépare 3 certificats à la Sorbonne etc etc etc . . . .

C Je le sais bien et puis si n'est pas lui qui a fait le voyage, cela revient peut-être au même: (gestes et sourires)

H Je ne comprends pas!

C Nous avons nos renseignements sur son activité politique; depuis quelques mois evidemment, il travaille et reste tranquille cela va mieux — c'est exact . . . .

Puis discussion sans intérêt sur la police ses informations avec une affirmation que la police russe a la tâche facile parce que dans ce pays tout le monde a la manie de la délation et de l'auto-accusation . . . etc (lieux communs) Puis confiance dans l'issue des élections nationales devant le péril allemand — Les allemands ces gens inassimillables que nous connaissons bien — Tous ces réfugés nous restons des ennemis pour eux; au premier appel ils iront reprendre leur fusil.

Comme vous le voyez les relations tout cordiales. Mais en ce qui concerne T tout est de la dépendance du ministre qui règle lui même "cette question." — (Je crois que cela est vrai)

[*May*] *16*

We are not cheerful these days. N. is unwell: temperature of 38° [C.] — apparently a cold, but there may also be malaria mixed in with it. Every time N. is ill, I feel anew the place that she fills in my life. She bears all suffering, physical as well as moral, silently, quietly, inside herself. Right now she is more upset about my health than her own. "If only you would get well," she said to me today, lying in bed, "that's the only thing I want." She rarely says such things. And she said this so simply, evenly, and quietly, and at the same time from such a depth, that my whole soul was stirred . . .

My condition is not encouraging. The attacks of illness have become more frequent, the symptoms are more acute, my resistance is obviously getting weaker. Of course, the curve may yet take a temporary turn upward. But in general I have a feeling that liquidation is approaching.

It's been about two weeks since I have written much of anything: it's too difficult. I read newspapers, French novels, Wittels' book about Freud (a bad book by an envious pupil), etc. Today I wrote a little about the interrelationship between the physiological determinism of brain processes and the "autonomy" of thought, which is subject to the laws of logic. My philosophical interests have been growing during the last few years, but alas, my knowledge is too insufficient, and too little time remains for a big and serious work . . .

I must give N. her tea . . .

May 17

Yesterday the papers published the official communiqué on the Laval negotiations in Moscow. Here is the most essential — the only essential — passage:

> Ils ont été pleinement d'accord pour reconnaître dans l'état actuel de la situation internationale, les obligations qui s'imposent aux Etats sincèrement attachés à la sauvegarde de la paix et qui ont clairement manifesté cette volonté de paix par leur participation à toutes recherches de garanties mutuelles, dans l'intérêt même du maintien de la paix. Le devoir, tout d'abord, leur incombe de ne laisser affaiblir en rien les moyens de leur défense nationale. A cet égard, M. Staline comprend et approuve pleinement la politique de défense nationale faite par la France pour maintenir sa force

armée au niveau de la sécurité. [*Clipping pasted in. The first sentence is crossed over vertically. The last two sentences are put in quotation marks and underlined by hand.*]

Even though I am sufficiently familiar with the political cynicism of Stalin, his contempt for principles, and his near-sighted practicality, I still could not believe my eyes when I read these lines. The cunning Laval has managed to find a way to approach that vain and limited bureaucrat. Stalin was undoubtedly flattered when a French minister asked him to pronounce his judgment on the armament of France: he did not even have the decency to separate his name from those of Molotov and Litvinov in this matter. The People's Commissar for Foreign Affairs was of course delighted by such an open and irreparable kick administered to the Comintern. Molotov may have been slightly embarrassed, but what does Molotov matter? His "relief" is already standing behind him, in the person of Chubar! And Bukharin and Radek, the official newspapermen, will interpret everything for the "people" in the proper fashion.

Nevertheless, Stalin will not live down the communiqué of May 15 with impunity. The question is too acute, and the treason is too barefaced. Precisely, treason! . . . After the capitulation of the German Communist Party to Hitler I wrote: This is the "Fourth of August" (1914) of the Third International. Some friends objected that the fourth of August had been treason, but here we had only capitulation. But the truth of the matter is precisely the fact that capitulation without a battle revealed an internal decay which inevitably precipitated the subsequent collapse. The communiqué of May 15 constitutes an act of treason in the fullest sense of the word, signed and notarized.

The French Communist Party has been mortally wounded. The miserable "leaders" had been reluctant to adopt openly a platform of social patriotism; they wanted to lead the masses up to capitulation imperceptibly and by degrees. Now their perfidious maneuver has been exposed. The proletariat will only gain from this. The cause of the new International will move forward.

A local doctor has been here to see N. *Grippe.* He found something in her lung, but N. said it was something old. But the "something old" (in Vienna) I think was in the left lung, and this time it is the right one. Although the doctor is a little man and superficial . . . Her temperature is about 38° [C.] all the time, and does not go down.

Their attitude toward the League of Nations best characterizes the left and leftward-moving reformists. The heads of the S.F.I.O. (Blum and Co.) once adopted — verbally — a program which maintains that it is necessary to smash the bourgeois "armature" of power, and to replace it by a worker-peasant state. At the same time Blum sees in the League of Nations the beginnings of a "democratic" international organization. How he plans to "smash" the national armature of the bourgeoisie and at the same time preserve its international organs — this would be a puzzle, if Blum were really planning to "smash" anything. In reality he intends to wait humbly for the bourgeoisie to smash its own "armature . . ." I must develop this idea.

[*A newspaper clipping follows.*]

DANS LES JOURNAUX

LES COMMUNISTES
FRANCAIS OBEIRONT-ILS A STALINE?

On sait que le communiqué final, qui a cloturé les entretiens de M. Laval avec Staline, Litvinoff et Molotoff "approuve pleinement la politique de défense nationale faite par la France pour maintenir sa force armée au niveau de la sécurité."

Il n'est pas sans intérêt de reproduire à ce sujet les commentaires des journaux du front commun. On remarquera que les explications de "L'Humanité" n'expliquent rien et que finalement, très embarrassés, les communistes français restent contre l'armée française . . .

L'HUMANITÉ (M. Magnien):

Staline a justement dit approuver les mesures de défense prises à l'égard des forces hitlériennes.

D'où peut venir le danger d'agression? Du fascisme hitlérien qui refuse de participer à toute mesure de paix, multiple les efforts vers Memel, vers l'Autriche, etc.

L'assistance mutuelle implique les mesures appropriées de défense de la paix. D'ailleurs, la politique de paix de l'Union soviétique, orientée vers les intérêts des masses travailleuses de l'U.R.S.S. comme de tous les pays, tend constamment au désarmement. L'organisation collective de la paix postule le désarmement, car la sécurité assurée pour tous, les conditions du désarmement général et simultané seront également assurées.

Quant à nous, communistes français, notre ligne de conduite n'en est pas modifiée. L'U.R.S.S. traite avec des gouvernements bourgeois, puisqu'elle est entourée de gouvernements bourgeois. Mais les travailleurs savent pertinément qu'ils ne peuvent se fier à leur bourgeoisie pour défendre la paix. [*The last two sentences are underlined in pencil.*]

Les communistes français, les travailleurs français ne peuvent pas avoir confiance dans les dirigeants de l'armée de la bourgeoisie française. Parmi les officiers de Weygand sont de nombreux fascistes, des hommes des Croix de feu et des hitlériens français. Tous les actes des fascistes français — que couvre le gouvernement français — prouvent que leur sympathies vont à Hitler, au fascisme allemand, principal fauteur de guerre en Europe.

Les communistes et les travailleurs français, qui mènent la lutte acharnée contre le fascisme, savent que ces hommes sont prêts à trahir le pacte franco-soviétique pour s'allier à Hitler contre l'U.R.S.S. La force que la France peut mettre au service de la défense de la paix, elle ne peut être sûre que sous la puissance de l'action des masses travailleuses, combattant sans répit contre le fascisme et la bourgeoisie, pour chasser de l'armée les officiers fascistes et réactionnaires. [*The last phrase is underlined in pencil.*]

Nous mettrons tout en œuvre pour défendre la paix, ainsi que son rempart, l'Union soviétique. C'est pourquoi nous continuerons à mettre tout en œuvre pour combattre les ennemis intérieurs de la paix et de l'U.R.S.S. contre les excitations chauvines qui sont le contraire de la défense de la paix et qui poussent à la guerre.

Tout pour la défense de la liberté et de la paix, tout pour la défense de l'U.R.S.S., pour le soutien de sa ferme politique de paix. Tout pour que le socialisme triomphant sur un sixième du globe soit victorieux du fascisme dans le monde. Voilà la lutte pour la paix poursuivie par les communistes.

LE POPULAIRE (Léon Blum):

Staline donne raison contre nous au gouvernement que nous avons combattu et dont le représentant à Moscou va revenir muni de son certificat de bonne conduite.

Il donne raison contre nous aux adversaires dont nous venons de soutenir le choc dans la récente bataille électorale.

Notre position, à nous, socialistes, qui, sans nier le devoir de défendre contre l'invasion le sol national, [*the last phrase underlined in pencil*] refusons cependant de nous solidariser avec les conceptions et l'organisation militaires de la bourgeoisie, est l'objet d'une condamnation.

Cette condamnation est implicite, mais elle est évidente.

Je crains que Staline n'ait pas, de Moscou, mesuré les répercussions que ces paroles [*the words* "Staline . . . paroles" *underlined in pencil*] exerceraient sur la situation politique en France, sur la situation prolétarienne en France.

LE PEUPLE (organe de la C. G. T.):

Il faut savoir que M. Laval a été exigeant et que Staline se moque éperdument du parti communiste français. Car celui-ci est aujourd'hui dans une position franchement ridicule.

Nous allons voir si les communistes sont des hommes libres ou si leur dépendance à l'endroit de Moscou est aussi intégrale que nous l'avons toujours dit. Nous tenons, pour notre part, qu'ils vont s'incliner platement devant l'ukase stalinien. Déjà, leur campagne contre les deux ans est radicalement stoppée.

Ainsi, à ce jour, Mussolini, Weygand, Laval et Staline sont d'accord pour affirmer publiquement que la sécurité des peuples repose, au premier chef, sur la qualité de leur armée. C'est au nom de cette politique révolutionnaire que les prolétaires français seront invités, l'un de ces jours, à revêtir l'uniforme pour la défense commune des privilèges de la bourgeoisie française et de la bureaucratie russe.

Mais les prolétaires français, et surtout les communistes français, marcheront-ils pour cette politique? Toléreront-ils qu'on se moque impunément d'eux, avec une désinvolture aussi characteristique?

Voici maintenant deux autres commentaires:

LE TEMPS:

Contre le dictateur révolutionnaire de Moscou, symbole et incarnation vivante du parti communiste russe, du communisme international, le parti socialiste se fait le champion du défaitisme, car le défaitisme consiste aussi à s'élever contre les moyens reconnus indispensables pour assurer la défense nationale et pour maintenir la force armée au niveau de la sécurité. Il s'agit de savoir si le parti radical peut tolérer désormais le moindre contact avec le défaitisme socialiste, avec l'antipatriotisme. Le pavé dans la mare aux grenouilles marxistes est aussi un pavé dans l'étang du cartel . . .

PARIS-MIDI (Marcel Lucain):

Reconnaissons sans passion et en toute impartialité que Staline vient de rendre le métier bien difficile aux révolutionnaires de chez nous. La France, certes, n'avait nul besoin de l'approbation d'un chef étranger, fût-il le dictateur des Soviets, pour comprendre son propre droit et son devoir de sécurité. Mais personne ne s'est trompé sur l'objectif exclusif du communiqué visant essentiellement à désavouer l'antimilitarisme et à infliger aux Blum et Cachin un démenti si cinglant à la face du monde que le front commun en serait désarticulé. Cette intention a d'ailleurs fait passer quel-que peu sur le caractère insolite d'une telle immixtion du chef du bolchevisme dans nos affaires les plus sacrées: une amitié, surtout lorsqu'elle est neuve, avec l'ardeur des premiers contacts, peut expliquer certaines audaces. Quoi qu'il en soit, M. Blum est à la fois désolé et indigné.

May 23

It has been quite a few days already that N. and I have been ill. Prolonged *grippe*. We stay in bed either by turns or together. May has been cold and dreary . . . Five days ago we received bad news from Paris: a taxi collided with a car in which Jeanne was riding and seriously injured her. She was taken to the hospital unconscious, with a deep gash in her head and broken ribs . . . Lyova is in the throes of studying for his examinations, and he has to cook for Seva. Still no news about Seryozha.

May 25

A letter from Lyova arrived today. As usual, it is written in veiled language:

"Je suis heureux de vous faire part que le conseil d'administration a voté à l'unanimité de donner l'autorisation en question. Il ne reste qu'à remplir des formalités. Dans 2 à deux jours et demi (peut être 3) nous aurons un texte que nous ferons parvenir aussitôt à Crux (pour signature). A ce moment là Crux recevra aussi toutes les détails sur l'affaire."

Affectueus . . .

L . . .

[*Piece of paper pasted in. Written in longhand.*]

This means that the Norwegian government has granted me a visa and that we should get ready to leave. "Crux" is myself. "A perpetual housewarming party," as an old workingman used to say in Alma-Ata.

May 26

The state of my health condemns me to reading novels. I picked up a book by Edgar Wallace for the first time. So far as I know he is one of the most popular authors in America and England. It is hard to imagine anything more mediocre, contemptible, and crude. Not a shade of perception, talent, or imagination. The adventures are piled on without any art at all, like police records laid one on top of the other. Not for a single moment did I feel any excitement, interest, or even simple curiosity. While reading the book you have a feeling as if out of boredom, for lack of anything better to do, you were drumming your fingers on a fly-specked windowpane . . .

By this book alone you can judge to what a degree enlightened England (and of course not England alone) remains a country of cultivated savages. It is the millions of Englishmen and Englishwomen who avidly and excitedly — to the point of fainting spells — gaped at the processions and solemnities of the jubilee of the royal couple, who are voracious readers of Wallace's products.

June 1935

June 1

The days drag by in burdensome succession. Three days ago we received a letter from our son: Seryozha has been arrested; he is in prison; now it is no longer guesswork, something almost certain but not quite; we have a direct communication from Moscow . . . He was arrested, evidently, about the time our correspondence stopped, i.e. at the end of December or the beginning of January. Almost half a year has elapsed since that time . . . Poor boy . . . And my poor, poor Natasha . . .

[*The following is a first draft of a letter in Mrs. Trotsky's hand, on paper torn out of a notebook, with many corrections and insertions. Some are in Trotsky's hand.*]

A letter by N. I. Trotskaya about her Son

Lately rumors have begun to circulate rather widely among our comrades that this time as the instrument of his revenge Stalin has selected our younger son Sergey. Friends have been inquiring of us: is it true? Yes, it is true. Seryozha was arrested at the very beginning of this year. If at first one could have hoped that the arrest was accidental and that my son would be freed any day, now it is quite evident that the intentions of the people who have arrested him are much more serious. Since many of our comrades take a vivid interest in this new blow that has fallen on our family, it might perhaps be good to describe the situation in a letter designed for general circulation.

Seryozha was born in 1909. He encountered the October Revolution as an eight-year-old boy and grew up in the Kremlin. In families where the adults are absorbed in politics, the younger members not infrequently shy away from politics. It was that way with us too. Seryozha was never concerned with political questions, and was not even a member of the Komsomol. During his school years he was enthusiastic about sports and circuses, and became an outstanding gymnast. In the university he concentrated in mathematics and mechanics; he was appointed by the Technical Institute as a teacher of engineering; during the last few years he has been very active in teaching, and recently published, in collaboration with two of his colleagues, a specialized work: *Light Generators of the Autotractor Type*. This book, which was published by the Scientific Autotractor Institute, received favorable notice from outstanding specialists.

When we were deported, Seryozha was still a student. The authorities permitted the members of our families the choice of accompanying us abroad or remaining in the U.S.S.R. Seryozha decided to stay in Moscow, so as not to tear himself away from the work which since that time has filled his whole existence. The material conditions of his life were very hard, but they did not differ in this respect from the living conditions of the overwhelming majority of Soviet young people who do not enjoy special privileges. The infamous slander which the Soviet press has been uninterruptedly spreading about L. D. Trotsky and his adherents could not fail, of course, to cause moral suffering to Seryozha. But about this I can only guess. My correspondence with my son has been limited exclusively to "neutral" everyday questions, never touching problems of politics or the special conditions of our family's existence. (I must add that even these letters reached their destination only in exceptional cases.) During the years of exile L. D. has not corresponded with his son at all, so as not to give the authorities the least pretext for persecution or petty harassment. And actually, during the six years of our present emigration, Seryozha has continued his intensive scientific and educational work without any hindrance on the part of the authorities.

The situation has changed since the murder of Kirov and the notorious trial of Zinoviev and Kamenev. The correspondence was broken off altogether. Seryozha was arrested. I waited day after day for the correspondence to be renewed. But now almost half a year has elapsed since Seryozha went to prison. This compels me to think that those who arrested him have some *special* intentions.

Is it possible to suppose that recent developments drew our son into working for the Opposition? I would be happy for him if I could think so, since under those conditions it would be immeasurably easier for Seryozha to bear the blow that has befallen him. But such a supposition must be altogether rejected. Various sources have informed us that Seryozha, during the last few years, kept as far away from politics as before. But personally I would not need even this evidence, since I know too well his psychology and the direction of his intellectual interests. And the authorities too, beginning with Stalin, are very well informed about that: indeed Seryozha, I repeat, grew up in the Kremlin; Stalin's son was a frequent guest in our boy's room; the G.P.U. and the University authorities watched him with redoubled attention later on, first when he was a student, then a young professor. He was arrested not for any oppositionist activity (which did not exist and, because of all the circumstances, could not have existed) but exclusively as the son of L. D., out of motives of blood vengeance. That is the only possible explanation.

All our comrades remember the attempt of the G.P.U. to inject the name of L. D. into the affair of Kirov's murder. The Lettish consul who gave money for the terroristic act at the same time made an offer to the terrorists to pass on a letter from them to Trotsky. All discussion of this project, however, was dropped in mid-air and only compromised the organizers of the trial. But exactly for this reason, after the trial we said in the family more than once: "They will not stop there; they will have to dig up some new affair in order to make up for the failure of the deal with the consul." L. D. also expressed the same idea in his articles in the Russian *Bulletin*. The only thing we did not know was what method the G.P.U. would select this time. But now there cannot be even a shadow of doubt: by arresting Sergey, who had no relation to the affair whatsoever, and by keeping him in prison for months, Stalin obviously and undoubtedly is pursuing the aim of creating a new "amalgam." For this, he needs to extract from Sergey some evidence, at the very least a "renunciation" of his father. I shall not speak about the methods by which Stalin succeeds in obtaining the testimony he needs. I have no information on this score. But all the circumstances speak for themselves . . .

It would be quite simple to verify what is said in this letter: it would suffice, for example, to create an international commission of authoritative and conscientious people, known, needless to say, to be friends of the U.S.S.R. Such a commission would have the duty of investigating all the repressions connected with the murder of Kirov; incidentally it would also throw the necessary light on the question of our son Sergey. There is nothing exceptional or unacceptable in such a proposal. In 1922, during the trial of the S[ocialist] R[evolutionaries] who had organized the attempt on the lives of Lenin and Trotsky, the Central Committee of the Bolshevik Party under the direction of Lenin and Trotsky offered to Vandervelde, Kurt Rosenfeld, and other *opponents* of the Soviet Government, the right to participate in the trial as defenders of the accused terrorists. This was done precisely in order to dispel any doubts whatever in the minds of the international proletariat as to the good faith and proper conduct of the trial. Couldn't Romain Rolland, Charles [*sic*] Gide, Bernard Shaw and other friends of the Soviet Union take the initiative to create such a commission by agreement with the Soviet Government? This would be the best method for investigating the truth of the accusations and the suspicions which are widespread among the working masses. The Soviet bureaucracy cannot stand above the public opinion of the working class of the world. As far as the interests of the workers' state are concerned, they would only profit by a serious examination of its actions. I, for one, would offer all the necessary information and documents concerning my son to such an authoritative commission. This letter of mine is at the same time a direct appeal to the labor organizations and foreign friends of the U.S.S.R., to those interested in being advocates of Soviet bureaucracy, and of course to the honest and independent friends of the October Revolution. If after long hesitation I openly raise the question of Sergey, it is not only because he is my son: that reason would be only too sufficient for a mother, but not adequate for setting in motion a political action. But Sergey's case is a completely clear, simple, and indisputable instance of conscious and criminal arbitrary abuse of power, and a case which can be examined very easily. The bureaucratic clique is oppressing and tormenting a Soviet worker known to be loyal, guilty of nothing, technically accomplished — only to satisfy the base instinct of revenge, and without the least political justification, since it is completely evident that attacking the son physically cannot exert any influence on the course of the father's political activity — activity with which Seryozha has never had the least connection. That is why I permit myself to think that the case of my son deserves public attention. In any case, if anyone intends to act he should act immediately, since if allowed to pass in silence and with impunity, the revengeful actions of Stalin may soon become irreparable.

June 1, 1935.

N. I. Trotskaya.

June 6

A prolonged governmental crisis. Just as once in Italy and later on in Germany, the parliament finds itself paralyzed at the most crucial moment. The immediate cause of this paralysis is the Radicals. Exactly for this reason, the Socialists and Communists are clinging to the Radicals with all their might . . . Our faction is growing. The slogan of the Fourth International is becoming almost fashionable. But the genuine, profound turn has not yet come . . .

June 8

L. S. [*name heavily inked out*], née Kliachko, the daughter of an old Russian emigré who died before the war, stopped in to see us on her way from London to Vienna. Her mother, an old friend of ours, has been in Moscow recently and apparently attempted to inquire into the fate of Seryozha, whom she had known as a little boy in Vienna. As a result, she had to leave Moscow in a great hurry. She does not know the details . . .

I received from a group of students of Edinburgh University, representing "all shades of political opinion," an offer to enter my candidacy for the post of Lord Rector. The post is purely "honorary" — the Lord Rector is elected every three years, publishes some sort of an address, and performs certain other symbolic actions. Among the former rectors they name: Gladstone, Smuts, Nansen, Marconi . . . Only in England, perhaps by now only in Scotland, would such an extravagant idea as entering my candidacy for the post of University Rector be possible. I answered, of course, with a friendly refusal.

[*Enclosure: letter draft, with many corrections and insertions*] I am very grateful to you for your unexpected and flattering proposal to enter my candidacy for the office of Lord Rector of the University of Edinburgh. The freedom from nationalistic considerations which is revealed in this offer does great honor to the spirit of the Edinburgh students. I appreciate your confidence all the more since, in your own words, you are not daunted by the refusal of the British Government to grant me a visa. However, I do not consider myself entitled to accept your offer. The election of the Lord Rector takes place, as you say, on an *apolitical basis,* and your letter is signed by representatives of all shades of political opinion. But I myself occupy too definite a political position: all my active life since my youth has been devoted to the revolutionary liberation of the proletariat from the yoke of capital. I have no other claim to occupy any responsible position. I would thus consider it treasonable to the working class and disloyal to you to appear in any public sphere under any but the Bolshevik banner. I do not doubt that you will find a candidate much better suited to the traditions of your university.

I wish you success in your enterprises with all my heart and remain gratefully

---

Externally everything in our home remains as before. But in actual truth everything has changed. Every time I recall Seryozha, it is with a sharp pain. But N. does not "recall" him, she always carries a deep sorrow inside her. "He put his trust in us . . . ," she said to me the other day (her voice still echoes in my heart) . . . "He thought that since we left him there, it was the way things had to be." And it has turned out that we have sacrificed him. That is just what it is . . .

Now, on top of this, my health has taken a sharp turn for the worse. This too N. takes very hard. One thing after another. Meanwhile she has to do a great deal of housework. Every day I am amazed anew: where does she get so much concentrated, passionate, and at the same time restrained energy?

S. L. Kliachko, our old Vienna friend, who thought very highly of N., once said that the only voice like hers that he had heard was Eleanora Duse's. (For S. L., Duse was the highest expression of the female personality.) But Duse was a tragic actress, while N. has nothing "theatrical" about her. She cannot "act," "perform a role," "imitate." She experiences everything with the utmost completeness and gives an artistic expression to her experiences. The secret of this artistry: depth, spontaneity, and wholeness of character.

Concerning the blows that have fallen to our lot, I reminded Natasha the other day of the life of the archpriest Avvakum. They were stumbling on together in Siberia, the rebellious priest and his faithful spouse. Their feet sank into the snow, and the poor exhausted woman kept falling into the snowdrifts. Avvakum relates:

And I came up, and she, poor soul, began to reproach me, saying: "How long, archpriest, is this suffering to be?" And I said, "Markovna, unto our very death." And she, with a sigh, answered: "So be it, Petrovich, let us be getting on our way." [*A small clipping, probably from a cheap edition, pasted in. Heavily underlined in pencil from the words* "How long" *to the end.*]

I can say one thing: never did Natasha "reproach" me, never — even in the most difficult hours; nor does she reproach me now, in the most sorrowful days of our life, when everything has conspired against us . . .

June 9

Van arrived yesterday and brought the news that the Norwegian Labor Government has granted the visa. Our departure from here is planned for tomorrow, but I don't think that in two days we shall succeed in getting a transit visa through Belgium: the boat leaves from Antwerp. Nevertheless, while waiting for the visa, we are packing. Unbelievable bustle. Everything happened at once: the peasant girl who used to come for three hours a day to help N. with the housework, as luck would have it, has left town on a visit for two days. Nat. cooks dinner, packs, helps me collect my books and manuscripts, and takes care of me. At least this distracts her somewhat from thoughts about Seryozha and the future. To add to all the rest, we are caught without any money: I have given too much time to party affairs, and in the last two months I was ill and in general worked badly. We shall arrive in Norway without any funds . . . But that, at all events, is the least of our worries.

A slight incident. Before our departure I had to have a haircut. In my situation this is a complex undertaking: I had to go to Grenoble with Van (it is two or three months since I had been to town). French barbers are very talkative, familiar, quick-witted — Figaro! My hair had grown very long, and I asked the barber to give me a short trim. My Figaro thought that was too short and would spoil my style, so to speak, but submitted. *"Bon,"* he said with obvious displeasure. When he had finished the job he said sententiously: "You look very different now; before you looked like Professor Piccard (the Belgian); now I wouldn't say so . . ." I asked him to *arranger* (fix up) my moustache. *"Raser?"* he asked with surprise: *"Tout à fait?"* There was an obvious suspicion in his voice. He had decided that I was trying to conceal my identity (which, by the way, is not so far from the truth). I reassured him: *"arranger, égaliser, non pas raser."* His garrulity came back right away. "But you wouldn't like it cut too short, à la Charlie Chaplin, would you? Of course not? By the way, one does not hear a thing about Chaplin since his *Lumières de la ville . . ."* And so on, and so on. Finally, when I, in answer to his question, replied that now everything was all right, he gave me his approval, not without a touch of irony: *"Comme client vous n'êtes pas difficile."* Even that is something!

[*End of Notebook 2*]

June 17

This is the second day we have been in Norway, in a country hotel, seventy kilometers from Oslo. Finland! Hills, lakes, pines, and firs . . . Only, the Norwegians are larger than the Finns. In their living conditions, I suppose, there is much that is primitive (even by comparison with France). But I should write it down in order.

June 20

On June 8 Van came to Domène to help us pack for the trip to Norway. The visa had not yet been received, i.e., had not yet been stamped in our passports, because of the Trinity holiday; but we had a telegram from Oslo to the effect that the Government had already reached a decision, and that the visa would be issued without hindrance after the holidays. N. was doubtful: wouldn't some new difficulties arise at the last moment, and wouldn't we be forced to get out of Paris again, since the authorities permitted us to stop in Paris only for twenty-four hours? We called Paris again on the telephone. Lyova answered that the visa was assured, that we would get it Tuesday morning, and that we should leave Monday. The packing went on feverishly; the main work fell on N., with Van helping her.

On Monday, the first thing in the morning, the director of the Grenoble *Sûreté* arrived at our house. An extremely disagreeable personage, with none of the French *courtoisie;* he called me *"Excellence"* for some reason — something the French have never done. He was ordered to accompany us to Paris. He explained to me in passing that he had spent two years in Russia, in the South, and had been in Odessa during the mutiny on the French ships: *"Vous connaissez — André Marty! . . . Moi, j'ai passé un mauvais quart d'heure."* There was nothing left for me to do but express my sympathy for him.

In Paris we were put up by Dr. R., who lives with his two sons — lawyers, the older one is a member of our organization. Tuesday morning H. M. went to the Norwegian consulate to get the visa; it turned out that they knew nothing about it. H. M. got in touch with our comrade in Oslo by telephone; he answered in a dejected voice that at the last moment the Government had begun to vacillate — wouldn't Tr. engage in revolutionary activity there? Furthermore, the Government could not answer for his safety . . . Departure on the first boat from Antwerp was out of the question. We had to start the arrangements virtually from the beginning. In the meantime our permit to stay in Paris was due to expire that evening. H. M. went to the *Sûreté nationale*. A stormy argument with the chief: Tr. has deceived us in order to be able to come to Paris! H. M. did a masterly job of negotiating with the authorities: if you raise a fuss you will scare the Norwegians; don't bother us, just give us some additional time, and we shall procure the visa. "Tr. must leave Wednesday evening; let him go to Belgium — he has a transit visa . . ." "But what will happen to him in Belgium?" "That is not our concern. You are reluctant to deceive Vandervelde, but you have deceived us . . ." H. M. proposed that while waiting for the visa Tr. could be put in a clinic. "In a clinic?! That is a classic maneuver! How shall we get him out of the clinic afterwards?" In conclusion these gentlemen gave H. M. to understand that a return to Domène (Isère) was impossible: the Minister Extraordinary of the Interior Paganon, deputy from Isère — a left Radical and consequently more cowardly than his predecessors — did not want to give his political adversaries grounds for accusing him of "giving refuge" to Trotsky in his Department . . .

The only thing left to do was to spend the forty-eight hours of grace putting pressure on Oslo. I got in touch by telephone with Scheflo, an editor in Christiansund, who warmly supported me in the matter of visa, sent a telegram to the Minister of Justice (on "noninterference" in politics and personal safety) and a second telegram to the Minister-President. Scheflo departed for Oslo by plane, so as to arrive in time for the meeting of the Council of Ministers on Wednesday evening. We had to cancel our tickets on the Norwegian boat by telephone. Meanwhile the Belgian transit visa had expired. Our young friends were in a very downcast mood . . .

In the meantime I was seeing numerous Parisian comrades. The worthy doctor's apartment had unexpectedly been transformed into the headquarters of the Bolshevist-Leninist faction. There were meetings going on in all the rooms, the telephones were ringing, more and more new friends kept arriving. The newspapers were full of reverberations from the Socialist congress in Mulhouse, and for the first time the attention of the big press centered upon the Trotskyists. "Putschists!" wrote *Le Temps,* at one with *L'Humanité*. Under these circumstances my stay in Paris must have made the police doubly nervous.

In Paris we saw Sevushka, after three years of separation. He has grown bigger and stronger, and . . . quite, quite forgot his Russian. The Russian book *Three Fat Men,* which in Prinkipo he used to read beautifully and avidly, he now approaches with distaste (although he has kept the book) as if it were something strange and worrying. He goes to a French school, where the boys call him a *boche* . . .

On Wednesday, at about half past nine in the evening, Held telephoned from Oslo that the Government had finally decided to grant me a visa for six months. "Six months" is a precautionary measure, so as not to have their hands tied in case of political opposition. The dejected mood of our young people was transformed into stormy enthusiasm . . .

Next morning, however, new difficulties cropped up. The Norwegian consul announced that since the visa was being granted for a definite period, Trotsky would need to have a return French visa; but he, the consul, would inquire about it in Oslo by telephone. There was almost no hope of obtaining a return French visa, and in any event it meant a considerable delay. More fuss, telephone conversations, excitement, and . . . expenses. By noon the Norwegian visa had been received, the Belgian transit visa extended to a new date. Last meetings and farewells. A new policeman to accompany us to Brussels.

We were accompanied to Antwerp, along with Van, by a French comrade named Rous from Perpignan, a Catalonian. The policeman who was escorting us proved to be a fellow countryman of his. They struck up an interesting conversation in the next compartment. The policeman usually votes for the Socialists. But confidence in the Socialists and Radicals among the police has waned: those parties do not want power and will not take it. The influence of the *Croix de Feu* has grown. The leftists say to the fascists: "But you don't have any program!" "That's nothing," the rightists answer: "First we must turn everything upside down, and then we shall see . . ." A beautiful formula for guardians of law and order! Lately sympathy for the Communists has been awakening among the police: they accept the need for national defense and at the same time are perhaps capable of showing some energy . . . Political polarization is thus going on even among the ranks of the French police. The hopes placed in Communist energy are of course illusory: precisely because they have recognized the need for national defense, they have cut themselves off from any possibility of revolutionary activity whatsoever. When a working-class party tells its bourgeoisie:

"Don't worry, we shall support you in case of war!" by this very act it terminates its existence as a revolutionary party.

We had to stay a day and a half in Antwerp. I took advantage of this to meet with our Belgian comrades. The leading group of five men — all workers — arrived from Charleroi. We gathered at the house of an Antwerp diamond worker, Polk (of the nationality and profession of Spinoza!), and spent about four hours in discussion.

On a small Norwegian boat (three nights and two days) nobody paid any attention to us. From that point of view the whole trip — unlike our previous migrations — was ideal. Neither the police nor the journalists nor the public took any interest in us. (N. and I traveled on *émigré* passports issued by the Turkish Government; since Van and Frankel were with us, the officer in charge of tickets and passports defined our group in this way: "A Frenchman, a Czechoslovak, and two Turks.") Only at the pier in Oslo did several journalists and photographers of the Labor — i.e., government — press divulge our incognito. But we departed quickly in a car with Scheflo, who was waiting for us on the pier.

The Government expressed the wish that we settle in the country outside of Oslo, about two hours' trip away. The newspapers discovered our retreat without any trouble. All in all, it caused a considerable sensation: the Norwegians were not expecting this visit in the least. But everything seems to promise to work out well. The conservatives are, of course, "indignant," but express their indignation in a comparatively restrained manner. The gutter press is maintaining neutrality. The Peasant Party, upon which — on the parliamentary plane — the very existence of the

Government depends, has not lodged any objections to the granting of my visa. The Labor press has rather firmly taken up the defense of the right of asylum, if not of me. The Conservatives wanted to raise a question in the Storting; but when they found they would get no sympathy from the other parties, they refrained. Only the fascists arranged a protest meeting under the slogan: "What does the leader of the world revolution want in Oslo?" Simultaneously the Stalinists announced for the thousand and first time that I was the leader of the world counterrevolution.

[*The following is a typewritten page, pasted in.*]

Die Arbeiterklasse des Landes und alle rechtdenkenden und vorurteilsfreien Menschen werden uebrigens den Beschluss, der Regierung freudig begruessen. Asylrecht soll kein toter Buchstabe, sondern eine Realitaet sein. Das norwegische Volk fuehlt sich darum auch nicht — wie Höire (die Konservativen) — beleidigt sondern geehrt durch Trotskis Aufenthalt hier im Lande.

Zu seiner Politik nehmen die norwegischen Arbeiter und ihre Partei nicht Standpunkt. Uns fehlen naemlich die Voraussetzungen dazu, uns eine gruendliche Meinung ueber den [Konflikt der] zwischen Stalin und Trotski entstanden ist, zu bilden. Es kann sein, das Stalin die Verhaeltnisse richtiger und realpolitischer gesehen hat als sein Rivale. [*The preceding section is marked off in the margin.*] Aber das berechtigt den siegenden Fluegel nicht, einen Mann wie Leo Trotski zu trakassieren und aus dem Lande zu weisen, einen Trotski, dessen Name in der Geschichte der russischen Revolution neben dem Lenins stehen wird. Wenn er trotz seiner grossen und unbestreitbaren Verdienste aus dem Lande gewiesen wird, muss es jedes demokratische Volk, als eine liebe Pflicht ansehen, ihm Behausung zu geben, besonders, wenn er noch dazu krank und niedergebrochen ist und einen Erholungsaufenthalt noetig hat.

Tranmael printed a very sympathetic article in the *Arbeiderbladet*. The most remarkable thing is that, while defending me against Stalin's persecutions, Tranmael unambiguously expresses his solidarity with the general policy of Stalin. This distribution of personal and political sympathies brings the necessary clarity to the problem.

* * *

Disturbing trials are now taking place in the U.S.S.R. The expulsion of Enukidze, the quietest and most pliant of men, is a blow at Kalinin. The justification for this — "Don't boast of your kindness!" — indicates the same thing. It will not be at all unexpected if this time Kalinin does not hold out. The day before yesterday there were telegraph reports of the murder of Antipov, the chairman of the Commission of Soviet Control. (There has been no confirmation.) The Central Committee demands that propagandists should not forget about Trotskyism, the Zinovievists, etc., even in the summer, during vacation. Nobody breathes a word about the glory of the Seventh Congress of the Comintern. Stalin's dictatorship is approaching a new frontier.

June 24

In the Storting there was a parliamentary "question" about me, not an interpellation. The presiding officer of the Storting made an ambiguous speech which disposed of the question. *Le Matin,* citing the German press, prints a report that several years ago I allegedly tried to enter Norway illegally, but was recognized on the border and not allowed to enter the country. The Moscow correspondent of the Conservative newspaper is warming over the Kirov case in connection with the Enukidze case . . . What does this mean?

Worst of all is the illness. Ten days of travel and living in hotels passed well, and I seemed to have revived. But now everything has come back at once: weakness, temperature, perspiration, inner physical emptiness . . . It's an affliction, there's no other word for it.

June 26

I go on being sick. It is amazing how much difference there is in me between health and sickness. I am like two different people, even in external appearance, and sometimes this happens within twenty-four hours. Hence there is a natural supposition that the cause is my nerves. But the physicians diagnosed an infection a long time ago, in 1923. It is possible that it is my "nerves" that give such a wide range to the external manifestations of the illness.

Last night, or rather early this morning, I dreamed I had a conversation with Lenin. Judging by the surroundings, it was on a ship, on the third-class deck. Lenin was lying in a bunk; I was either standing or sitting near him, I am not sure which. He was questioning me anxiously about my illness. "You seem to have accumulated nervous fatigue, you must rest . . ." I answered that I had always recovered from fatigue quickly, thanks to my native *Schwungkraft,* but that this time the trouble seemed to lie in some deeper processes . . . "Then you should *seriously* (he emphasized the word) consult the doctors (several names) . . ." I answered that I already had many consultations and began to tell him about my trip to Berlin; but looking at Lenin I recalled that he was dead. I immediately tried to drive away this thought, so as to finish the conversation. When I had finished telling him about my therapeutic trip to Berlin in 1926, I wanted to add, "This was after your death"; but I checked myself and said, "After you fell ill . . ."

N. is fixing up our living quarters. How many times she has done this! There are no wardrobes here, and many other things are lacking. She is hammering nails in by herself, stringing cords, hanging things up and changing them around; the cords break; she sighs to herself and begins all over again. She is guided in this by two considerations: cleanliness and attractiveness. I remember with what heartfelt sympathy — almost tenderness — she told me in 1905 about a certain fellow prisoner, a common criminal, who had "understood" cleanliness and helped N. to clean up their cell. How many "furnishings" we have changed in thirty-three years of living together: a Geneva *mansarde,* flats in the working-class districts of Vienna and Paris, and the Kremlin and Arkhangelskoe, a peasant hut near Alma-Ata, a villa in Prinkipo, and much more modest villas in France . . . N. has never been *indifferent* to her surroundings, but always *independent* of them. I easily "let down" under difficult conditions: that is, become reconciled to the dirt and disorder around me, but N. — *never.* She raises every environment to a certain level of cleanliness and orderliness, and does not allow it to fall below that level. But how much energy, inventiveness, and vital forces it requires! . . .

I lie down now for days at a time. Today N. and I were arranging a chaise longue behind the barn. "Do you want it this way?" she asked me with a shade of regret. "Why?" "The view is better on the other side." Indeed, the view was incomparably better on the opposite side. Of course anyone, or almost anyone, can tell a better view from an inferior one. But N. cannot help feeling the difference with her whole being. She cannot sit down facing a fence, and suffers with pity if somebody else faces that way.

N. and I have lived a long and hard life together, but even now she does not cease to *amaze* me by the unspoiled, integral, artistic quality of her nature.

Lying on my chaise longue, I remembered how N. and I had been subjected to a sanitary inspection aboard ship when we arrived in New York in January, 1917. American officials and doctors are very unceremonious, especially with passengers not in the first class — we were traveling second class. Natasha was wearing a veil. The doctor, thinking of trachoma, suspected something wrong behind the veil, quickly lifted it up and made a move with his fingers to lift up her eyelids . . . N. did not protest, said nothing, did not step back; she was just surprised. She glanced at the doctor questioningly and blushed a little. But the coarse Yankee immediately dropped his hands and stepped back apologetically: there was such an irresistible dignity of womanhood in her face, in her glance, in her whole figure . . . I remember what a feeling of pride in Natasha I had as we walked down the ramp to the New York pier.

June 29

There is a long letter from some lawyer in *Aftenposten:* Trotsky never renounced his political activity (my letter to the Edinburgh students is cited in particular); besides, he has two secretaries. What are they planning to do if he is sick? The same author refers to the statement by Scheflo that Trotsky is "not broken," "remains what he was," etc. Evidently one cannot manage to achieve oblivion even here.

I am trying to overcome my illness by "slow starvation." I lie in the shade, read almost nothing, think almost nothing.

July 1935

July 1

Lying in the open air, I looked through a collection of articles by the anarchist Emma Goldman with a short accompanying biography, and am now reading the autobiography of "Mother Jones" [*in English*]. They both came from the ranks of American working women. But what a difference! Goldman is an individualist, with a small "heroic" philosophy concocted from the ideas of Kropotkin, Nietzsche and Ibsen. Jones is a heroic American proletarian, without doubts or rhetoric, but also without a philosophy. Goldman sets herself revolutionary aims, but tries to achieve them by completely unrevolutionary means. Mother Jones always sets herself the most moderate aims: *more pay and less hours* [in English], and tries to achieve them by bold and revolutionary means. They both reflect America, each in her own way: Goldman by her primitive rationalism, Jones by her no less primitive empiricism. But Jones represents a splendid landmark in the history of her class, while Goldman signifies a departure from her class into individualistic nonexistence. I could not stomach the Goldman articles: lifeless moralizing which smacks of rhetoric, despite all its sincerity. I am reading the Jones autobiography with delight.

In her terse and completely unpretentious descriptions of strikers' battles, Jones incidentally reveals a horrifying picture of the underside of American capitalism and its democracy. It is impossible to read without shudders and curses her tales of the exploitation and maiming of young children in the factories!

Knudsen informs me that the fascists are organizing in Drammen (sixty kilometers from here) a meeting of protest against my stay in Norway. According to K. they will not collect more than a hundred people.

Some Soviet official has rented a cottage in the vicinity of the little summer cottage of our landlord. This worries N., but I think without any foundation.

July 4

I have finished reading the autobiography of Mother Jones. It has been a long time since I have read anything with such interest and excitement. An epic book! What unflagging devotion to the working people, what organic contempt for the traitors and careerists from among the working-class "leaders." With ninety-one years of life behind her, this woman at a Pan-American Workers' Congress held up the example of Soviet Russia. At ninety-three she joined the Farmer-Labor Party. But the main substance of her life was her participation in workers' strikes, which — in America more frequently than anywhere else — turned into civil war . . . Has this book been translated into foreign languages?

July 13

During the daytime lately I have been lying in the open air, reading and dictating letters to Jan. Newspapers and letters have begun arriving here directly and in ever-increasing numbers.

A few days ago our landlord had guests, also party

editors; they came here to make our acquaintance. "Fascism cannot happen in Norway." "We are an old democracy." "We have complete literacy." "Besides we have learned a lot: we have limited our capitalism . . ." And if fascism conquers in France? In England? "We shall hold out." Why then did you not hold your currency when it fell in England?

They have learned nothing. Essentially, these people do not suspect that such men as Marx, Engels and Lenin have lived in this world . . . The war and the October Revolution, the upheavals of fascism, have passed them by without a trace . . . For them, the future holds hot and cold showers.

I have read the biography of Eugene Debs. The biography is bad, lyrically sentimental; but in its way it reflects the lyrical and sentimental figure of Debs, remarkable of its kind, and in any case very attractive.

I am reading Edgar Allan Poe in the original, and am getting on, although not without difficulties. In recent years I have learned to dictate articles in French and German, to dictate to collaborators who are capable of correcting my syntactic errors on the spot. The latter are not infrequent. It has not been given to me to master *completely* any foreign language.

In English (which I know quite badly) I am making progress now with the help of intensive reading. Sometimes I catch myself wondering: isn't it a bit too late? Is it worth while to expend this energy not on knowledge, but on language, a tool of knowledge?

In Turkey we lived "openly" under the public eye, but actually under a considerable guard (three comrades and two policemen). In France we lived incognito, first under a guard of our comrades (Barbizon), later alone (Isère). Now we are living openly and without guard. Even the yard gate is wide open day and night. Yesterday two drunken Norwegians dropped in to get acquainted. We chatted with them amiably and parted.

July 30

There have been many minor events during the last two weeks. Tranmael, the chief of the Party, and Lie, the Minister of Justice, came to make our acquaintance. It happened that we were photographed together (at the insistence of a naïve third person). I thought of the joint photograph with anxiety. But — luckily — the photograph was not at all suitable for the minister either. Two or three days later we were informed that the picture "did not come out." N. and I were very pleased with the resourcefulness of our important guests. The conversation turned out to be one-sided: the editor of the central organ of the Party "interviewed" me in the presence of Tranmael (the chief editor) and Lie. We spent the time pleasantly. Lie assured us that the Soviet Government had not brought any pressure to bear to prevent my settling in Norway. They apparently did not know anything about it until the day we arrived in Oslo. It is also possible that they considered Norway a lesser evil than France. In the *Arbeiderbladet* they printed a very belligerent article.

The other day a fascist journalist (from the weekly magazine *ABC*) stole into our yard; he crept up along the wall and snapped N. and me on our chaises longues. When N. turned toward him, he took to his heels. It is a good thing that it was only a camera he had in his hands. Jan caught up with him in the village, where he was calling for an automobile by telephone. The poor fascist trembled from fear, swore that he had not taken any pictures, etc. But the photographs did appear in *ABC* with a threatening article: are the police taking notice of the destructive activity of Tr[otsky]? The snapshot does not justify this tone: we are lying peacefully on our folding chairs . . .

The day before yesterday two brothers, workers or rather, small entrepreneurs, builders, came from Oslo. They have lived in America, speak English, are not young. They sympathize with the Comintern, belong to the Society of "Friends of the U.S.S.R." The argument turned out to be long and not very coherent (because of the language barrier). But the type of Norwegian "Stalinist" displayed itself for me completely.

Just received a telegram: our young people have been expelled from the [French] Socialist Party: this is the price of the forthcoming merger of the Social Democrats with the Stalinists. A new chapter is commencing.

September 1935

September 8

I have not written anything for a long time. A doctor has been here from R[eichenberg, Czechoslovakia] to treat me, very friendly, "ours." Made me walk a great deal in order to test the course of the disease. My condition became worse right away. Analyses, as usual, did not show anything. Two weeks passed this way. After the doctor's departure I reverted to a recumbent mode of living and soon recovered. I have begun to work, more and more. We found a Russian typist, which is my salvation, in the literal sense of the word. I began to dictate — a great deal, easily, almost without fatigue. I find myself in this condition right now. That is why I forgot even to think about the diaries.

I remembered them because yesterday we received from Lyova copies of letters from Aleksandra Lvovna and Platon. Not a word from Seryozha or about Seryozha: it is very probable that he is still in prison . . .

The letters of Al. Lvovna and Platon speak for themselves.

[*Enclosure: a typewritten page.*]

14.8.35

Dear Lyova,

I had been much worried by the absence of letters from you. But finally the news about Sevushka arrived. How good it is that he is with you now, that little boy. His father is in Omsk, and has inquired about his little son. You should write to him, for the time being, care of General Delivery. It seems to me that you cannot have received my last letter. I wrote you that Nina's children are living with my sister in *Kirovo, Ukraine* [underlined by hand].

My sister is a very sick person, and I don't know how she managed to move there all alone, without any help. Her address is: *Kirovo, Odessa Region, 4 Karl Marx Street, apt. 13.* The children have kept hoping for a meeting with their father (Man) soon, but they will have to wait *two years* [underlined by hand] more. I am very much touched, as always, by your thoughtful attitude toward me. There is no point in sending money to me — there is no place to cash it here. All my needs are satisfied by parcels from my sister. Here one can get hardly anything, not even vegetables. My health is so-so. I hope to have a chance to see the children again — that is, not to die before then. There is no point, of course, in mentioning how I feel. But I have great endurance, and hope that even now I shall not change.

Platon begs earnestly for a picture of Sevushka. I was about to send it to him, although I hate to part with it. Now I hope that you will send him one directly. Hasn't Sevushka forgotten his Russian? And does he remember us? Give him a big kiss for me. Where is Sergey?
Love and embraces, Yours, Aleks.

1.8.35.
My dears,
Up to now there has been no word from you, except for a single message with a check on Torgsin dated March. But the check is still traveling back and forth; quite possibly it will be found to have expired, and I shall probably return it to you. There have been no letters at all from my little son. I received notices of the arrival of some letters at the old place, but don't know how it will work out here; perhaps some day I shall at last receive from you news of my little boy. Too bad you sent me such a big check; it would have been better to parcel it out in at least ten or fifteen parts; that would have been enough for me, and it would have been better. There is a Torgsin here. If I manage to cash the old check after all its travels, I shall share it with Grandmother, who is not here now, as I had thought she was, but in the Uvat District. *My health is improving little by little, but generally speaking the fact that I am here — for five years — is quite unexpected* [underlined by hand]. I am starting a new phase, after having been on the

road of the old Lafargues and having almost joined our Zinushka. Warm greetings from me and all best wishes. I hope that you will comfort me with news of Sevik, his health, studies, pranks. So far I don't know anything about his photograph; it's very hard. Warm love to the boy and all of you.

Yours, P.

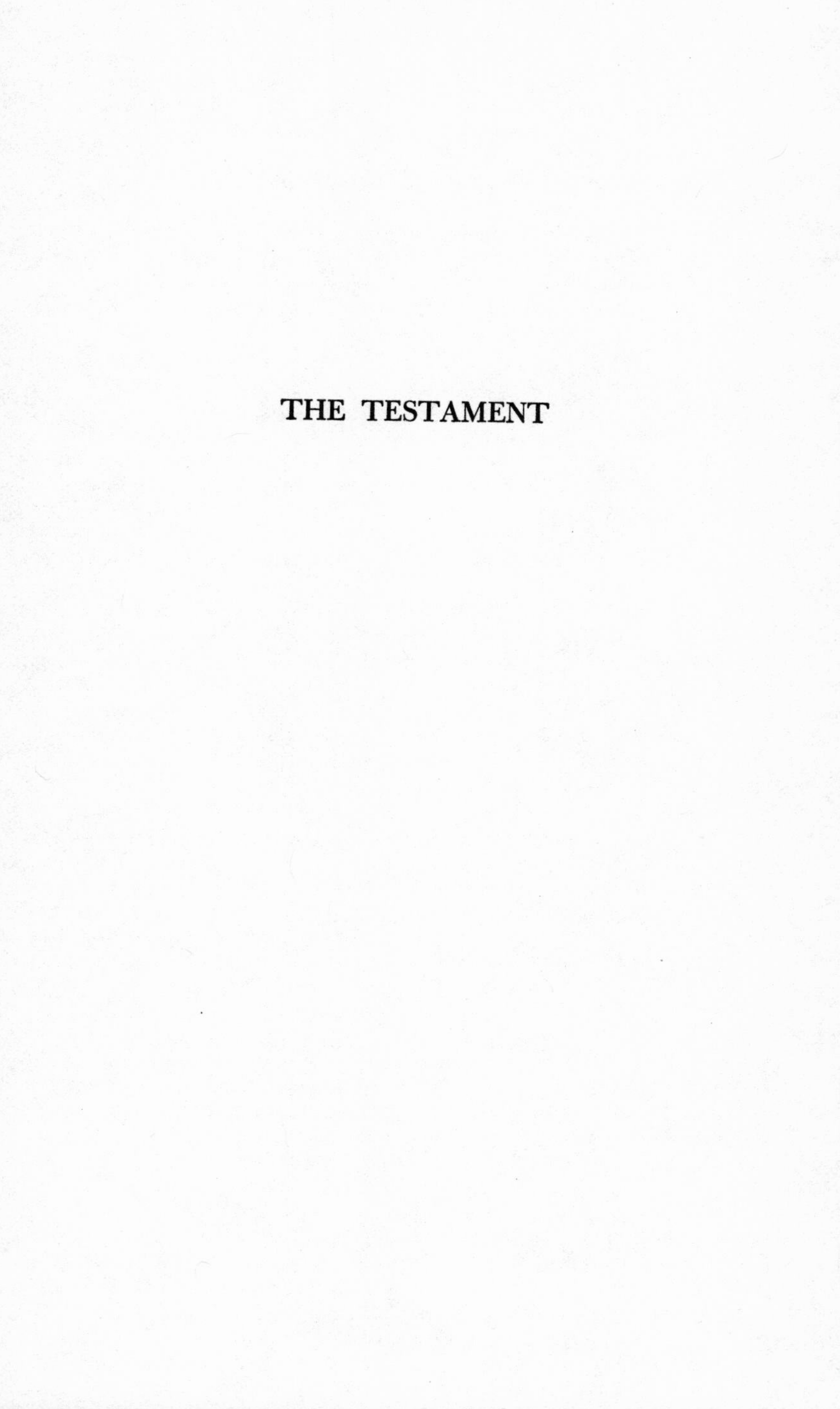

THE TESTAMENT

TESTAMENT

My high (and still rising) blood pressure is deceiving those near me about my actual condition. I am active and able to work but the outcome is evidently near. These lines will be made public after my death.

I have no need to refute here once again the stupid and vile slander of Stalin and his agents: there is not a single spot on my revolutionary honor. I have never entered, either directly or indirectly, into any behind-the-scenes agreements or even negotiations with the enemies of the working class. Thousands of Stalin's opponents have fallen victims of similar false accusations. The new revolutionary generations will rehabilitate their political honor and deal with the Kremlin executioners according to their deserts.

I thank warmly the friends who remained loyal to me through the most difficult hours of my life. I do not name anyone in particular because I cannot name them all.

However, I consider myself justified in making an exception in the case of my companion, Natalia Ivanovna Sedova. In addition to the happiness of being a fighter for the cause of socialism, fate gave me the happiness of being her husband. During the almost forty years of our life together she remained an inexhaustible source of love, magnanimity, and tenderness. She underwent great sufferings, especially in the last period of our lives. But I find some comfort in the fact that she also knew days of happiness.

For forty-three years of my conscious life I have remained

a revolutionist; for forty-two of them I have fought under the banner of Marxism. If I had to begin all over again I would of course try to avoid this or that mistake, but the main course of my life would remain unchanged. I shall die a proletarian revolutionist, a Marxist, a dialectical materialist, and, consequently, an irreconcilable atheist. My faith in the communist future of mankind is not less ardent, indeed it is firmer today, than it was in the days of my youth.

Natasha has just come up to the window from the courtyard and opened it wider so that the air may enter more freely into my room. I can see the bright green strip of grass beneath the wall, and the clear blue sky above the wall, and sunlight everywhere. Life is beautiful. Let the future generations cleanse it of all evil, oppression, and violence and enjoy it to the full.

L. Trotsky

February 27, 1940
Coyoacan.

TESTAMENT

All the possessions remaining after my death, all my literary rights (income from my books, articles, etc.) are to be placed at the disposal of my wife, Natalia Ivanovna Sedova. February 27, 1940. L. Trotsky.

In case we both die [*The rest of the page is blank.*]

March 3, 1940

The nature of my illness (high and rising blood pressure) is such — as I understand it — that the end must come suddenly, most likely — again, this is my personal hypothesis — through a brain hemorrhage. This is the best possible end I can wish for. It is possible, however, that I am mistaken (I have no desire to read special books on this subject and the physicians naturally will not tell the truth). If the sclerosis should assume a protracted character and I should be threatened with a long-drawn-out invalidism (at present I feel, on the contrary, rather a surge of spiritual energy because of the high blood pressure, but this will not last long), then I reserve the right to determine for myself the time of my death. The "suicide" (if such a term is appropriate in this connection) will not in any respect be an expression of an outburst of despair or hopelessness. Natasha and I said more than once that one may arrive at such a physical condition that it would be better to cut short one's own life or, more correctly, the too slow process of dying . . . But whatever may be the circumstances of my death I shall die with unshaken faith in the communist future. This faith in man and in his future gives me even now such power of resistance as cannot be given by any religion.

L. Tr

NOTES

NOTES

The notes that follow deal with all the names or historical events mentioned in the Diary, with the exception of those that are generally familiar or of names that are identified in the Diary itself.

February 7

Where asterisks or elliptical dots appear in the text, they are Trotsky's own punctuation; nothing has been omitted.

Ferdinand Lassalle (1825–1864), friend and for a time disciple of Marx and Engels, founded the General German Workers' Union, the first significant German socialist organization.

February 8

Léon Blum (1872–1950) became prominent in the French Socialist Party after World War I. In 1936 he became Premier of the first Popular Front government. "Today's issue" refers to Blum's newspaper, *Le Populaire* (sometimes abbreviated *"Popu"*), the daily organ of the Socialist Party, published in Paris.

On February 6, 1934, a loose coalition of French right-wing, nationalist, and veterans' organizations mobilized about the Chamber of Deputies in a violent but unsuccessful effort to force the overthrow of the Daladier government.

Pierre-Etienne Flandin (1889–1958) was the leader of the "Left Republicans," one of the center groups in the Chamber of Deputies. He became Minister of the Interior and, for six months, Premier. Marcel Cachin (1869–1958) led the extreme right wing of the French Socialist Party during World War I, turned Communist after the Bolshevik Revolution, and was for a long time spokesman for the Communist parliamentary group in the Chamber of Deputies. He was a strong partisan of the Stalin wing in the fight against Trotsky.

L'Humanité (abbreviated *"Huma"*), earlier the most influential daily newspaper of the French Socialist Party, was taken over in 1920 by the newly-formed French Communist Party to become its official organ.

Victor Adler (1852–1918) was from 1889 to 1918 the leader of the Social Democratic Party of Austria; he played a major role in the prewar Socialist International.

Le Temps, widely regarded as the unofficial voice of most of the governments of France, was one of the most influential newspapers of its day; Trotsky, however, considered it to be very corrupt.

February 9

Matyas Rakosi (1892–1971) was one of the leaders of the short-lived Hungarian Soviet Republic in 1919, and then a leader of the Hungarian Communist Party; he was active in the fight against Trotsky. Trotsky refers here to Rakosi's trial and the sentence of life imprisonment imposed on Rakosi for illegal communist agitation. Until 1956, Rakosi was chief of state of the Hungarian "People's Republic."

Grigori Zinoviev (Hirsch Apfelbaum, 1883–1936) was one of Lenin's right-hand men in the period of exile between the revolutions of 1905 and 1917, becoming in 1919 the first leader of the Communist International. One of the first leaders in the fight against "Trotskyism" in 1923, Zinoviev nevertheless later established with Trotsky a bloc against Stalin. In 1928, he capitulated to Stalin, on threat of expulsion from the Communist Party, and in 1936, in the first of the Moscow "Show Trials," was tried, condemned, and executed.

Nicholas Horthy (Miklos Horthy de Nagybanya, 1868–1957), Admiral under the Austro-Hungarian monarchy and Regent of

Hungary after the Communist government fell in 1919, ruled Hungary as military dictator until 1944.

Louis-Oscar Frossard, with Marcel Cachin, led the French Socialist Party after World War I, when they helped to swing the party to affiliation with the Communist International. After a brief period in the new Communist Party, he returned to the Socialist Party and became an associate of Léon Blum.

February 11

Ernst Röhm, organizer and leader of the Nazi Storm Troops, was executed by Hitler's orders in the first "purge" inside the Nazi Party. He and his associates were charged with immorality and disloyalty. The Mensheviks (literally, "supporters of the Minority, *menshinstvo*") and the Bolsheviks ("supporters of the Majority, *bolshinstvo*") originally were the two disputing factions at the Second Congress of the Social Democratic Labor Party of Russia in London in 1903. At that time the Bolsheviks were led by Lenin, and the Mensheviks by L. (Julius) Martov (Julius Ossipovich Tsederbaum, 1873–1923). After the formal split of the party in 1912, Martov led the Menshevik, or Social Democratic, Party. A vigorous critic of the Bolsheviks, he died in exile.

Translation of Röhm: "Flaming protests and mass meetings are certainly valuable for producing a mood of exaltation and often, perhaps, they are even indispensible; but if there is no man on hand who makes, behind this smoke screen, practical preparations for action, and is determined to act, they have no effect."

February 12

Paul Vaillant-Couturier, editor of *L'Humanité,* formerly head of the left-wing war veterans' association, was one of the leaders of the French Communist Party during this period. Wilhelm Gröner (1867–1939) had been high on the German general staff and the German War Office during World War I, but had resigned in protest against the signing of the Treaty of Versailles. He later served as the Weimar Republic's Minister of the Interior.

Translation of Röhm: "But only the uniforms and insignia had disappeared. Just as before, the Storm Troops trained on the maneuvering grounds at Doeberitz as on other training grounds owned by the government of the Reich. Only now they did not appear as the Storm Troops, but as the German Popular Sport Society."

The "Proudhonist-Anarchist Congress" opened in Brussels on September 7, 1874, as the "Seventh General Congress of the International Workingmen's Association." Its participants were mainly followers of the French socialist, Pierre Joseph Proudhon (1809–1865), and strong opponents of "authoritarian socialists," as exemplified to them by Marx and Engels.

Engels, translated: "General disunity about all essentials is concealed by the fact that they don't debate, but only talk and listen." Friedrich Sorge, German socialist, was a friend and follower of Marx and Engels. After being active in the labor movement in the United States, Sorge was appointed Secretary of the International Workingmen's Association (the "First International," founded 1864).

The "London-Amsterdam bloc" refers to a loose grouping in the mid-thirties of Socialist Parties belonging to neither the Second nor the Third International.

The Jeunesses Patriotes was a paramilitary organization, composed largely of university students of clerical and extremely nationalist inclination; it participated actively in the riots of February 6, 1934.

The reference to "Notre-Dame" apparently has to do with the fact that Flandin had recently attended a religious ceremony in the Cathedral of Notre-Dame.

V. B. Chubar, previously Chairman of the Council of People's Commissars of the Ukrainian Soviet Socialist Republic, was promoted to an important Party post in Moscow during the period of Stalin's rise. Jan Rudzutak, a member of the Bolshevik Party, was active in the trade-union movement. After the Russian Revolution, he held various posts high in the Communist Party. Initially a partisan of Stalin, he was executed in one of the Party's purges. Valery Mezhlauk, one of the members of the Council of War and later a leader in the work of economic reconstruction after the Bolshevik Revolution, rose to prominence under Stalin. However, he disappeared from the political scene without official announcement during the thirties.

The remark about the petty bourgeois was provoked by Trotsky's difficulties with his French landlord.

February 13

Marcel Régnier was Minister of the Interior in the Flandin cabinet.

Trotsky lived at Prinkipo ("Isle of Princes"), a Turkish island in the Sea of Marmora, after his banishment from Russia in 1929.

Maurice Thorez (1900–1964) was a former mine worker who rose to prominence in the French Communist Party after the replacement of its original leadership in the early thirties. He became General Secretary of the Party.

February 14

Florence Kelley Wischnewetsky, an American socialist and reformer, translated Engels' *The Condition of the Working Class in England in 1844,* and corresponded with Engels for many years. James Ramsay MacDonald (1866–1937), at one time leader of the British Labour Party, was several times Prime Minister of England.

The "veritable plot" probably refers to the following situation.

On Trotsky's initiative, the French Trotskyist organization dissolved as an independent organism, and all its members joined the Socialist Party or the Socialist Youth, in order to influence the course of the socialist organizations to the left and to provide a bulwark against the infiltration of the Communists and their ideas. For a while, the Trotskyists recorded some success, especially among the Socialist Youth. The more conservative sections of the Socialist Party were disturbed at the progress of the Trotskyists and began to consider organizational means against them within the Party. The Communist press launched a systematic campaign, calling upon the Socialists to expel the Trotskyists as "Social Fascists," "enemies of unity," and so on. Finally, the Trotskyists were expelled, and formed an independent party of their own.

Nikolai Bukharin (1888–1938), Bolshevik party leader, was regarded next after Lenin as the outstanding Party theoretician. For many years member of the Political Bureau and editor of *Pravda,* he was closely associated with Stalin against Trotsky and Zinoviev. In 1928, Bukharin broke with Stalin over questions of national economic policy and party politics, to form, with Aleksey Rykov and M. P. Tomsky, the "Right Opposition." Bukharin was expelled from the Communist Party in 1929, recanted, and in 1934 was appointed editor of *Izvestia,* from which he was dismissed ten months later. Charged with counterrevolutionary activity, he was executed after the Moscow Trial of 1938.

Aleksandr Kerensky (1881–1970) was one of the socialist leaders of the revolution of February, 1917. He held various offices in the provisional government, ending as Prime Minister at the time of the Bolshevik Revolution. The reference here is to the brief alliance between Kerensky and Irakly Tseretelli, a leader of the Menshevik wing of the Russian Social Democratic Party. Tseretelli had been a member of the pre-Revolution Duma, the provisional government, and the All-Russian Soviet under Menshevik and Socialist Revolutionary leadership. Tseretelli strongly opposed the Bolshevik Revolution.

"S.F.I.O." (Section Française de l'Internationale Ouvrière) is the Socialist Party of France; "C.G.T." (Confédération Générale du Travail) is the national French trade-union organization.

Ernst Thälmann was the pro-Stalin leader of the German Communist Party during the late twenties and early thirties.

Albert Oustric was a French banker, whose speculations ended in 1930 in a crash that ruined several banks, wiped out the savings of small investors to the amount of about one and one half billions of francs, and involved several important government officials in scandal, helping to cause the fall of the Tardieu cabinet. Serge Alexandre Stavisky, the financier, died in January, 1934, under mysterious circumstances. His death, at a time of social discontent, provoked rumors of scandal involving police and government officials, and the political storm that arose around *"l'affaire* Stavisky" was utilized by the promoters of the riots on February 6, 1934.

The Comité des Forges, the famous association of iron, steel, and coal interests, exercised a strong influence on the economic and political life of France. Havas was the semiofficial agency for gathering and distributing news in France. The incident, which occurred in Grenoble, had been described to Trotsky by friends there. The De Wendel family controls one of the oldest, largest, and most powerful French metallurgical enterprises.

Leonid Krassin (1870–1926), a distinguished engineer and active revolutionary in tsarist Russia, became one of the most effective diplomatic representatives abroad of the Soviet Government.

A. Rafalovich, secret councillor of the Russian Ministry of Finance in Paris before World War I, was charged with bribing French journalists and publishers to support the tsarist government and its foreign policy and requests for French loans. His letters to tsarist ministers in Russia on the sweeping extent of his successes with the French press were made public after the Bolshevik Revolution.

The Latvian consul was cited by the Soviet press as the alleged intermediary between Trotsky and the killer of Sergey Kirov, a leader in the Stalin government and chief of the Leningrad organization of the Russian Communist Party. Kirov's assassination, in December, 1934, touched off a prolonged series of trials and blood purges throughout the Soviet Union. Neither the consul nor the Latvian Government was mentioned during the proceedings of the trial, in 1936, of the defendants, who were charged with various other crimes as well as the assassination.

Lev Kamenev (Rosenfeld) (1883–1936) was a Bolshevik leader from 1914 on. He was an intimate friend and colleague of Lenin and always closely associated with Zinoviev. He was one of the principal defendants in the Moscow Trials of 1936.

Grigori Evdokimov was the official Bolshevik Party orator at Lenin's funeral. Associated with the Zinoviev Opposition (to Stalin), Evdokimov was a codefendant at the 1936 Moscow Trials.

Translation of Engels (from a letter to Friedrich Sorge): "In France the Radicals in the government are making fools of themselves more than one could have hoped. Where the workers are concerned, they are repudiating their own old program *in toto* and appear as sheer opportunists. They are pulling the opportunists' chestnuts out of the fire and washing their dirty linen. That would be splendid, if Boulanger didn't exist and they weren't chasing the masses, almost by main force, into his arms." Georges Ernest Jean Marie Boulanger (1837–1891) was a noted French general who led a movement in the eighties to replace the French Republic with a "popular" dictatorship. When the government took measures toward procuring his arrest, he left France.

The *Parti Radical et Radical-Socialiste,* commonly called the Radicals, is now neither radical nor socialist by American political definition. Republican and secular, it occupies a center position embracing a wide range of political tendencies, and thus has often been able to govern in coalition with elements close to it at both ends.

The "madhouse at Charenton" is the well-known Hospice de Charenton, actually at St. Maurice, not far from Paris.

The Popular Front was the name given to the bloc formed in 1935 by the Radical, Socialist, and Communist parties for the defense of the French Republic from the threat of fascist organizations.

The German quotation — "Reason becomes nonsense, a good deed — a curse!" — is from Goethe's *Faust,* I, 1. 1976.

Paul Faure was at this time General Secretary of the Socialist Party. Jean Zyromsky was one of the spokesmen for the left wing of the Socialist Party, especially in the Paris region. He was a Communist sympathizer, and finally joined that party during World War II. For Vaillant-Couturier, see note under February 12.

February 15

The *Bulletin of the Opposition,* Trotsky's principal organ in exile, was a monthly review in the Russian language. It appeared first in Berlin and then in Paris under the editorship of Trotsky and his son, Leon Sedov, and, before publication was suspended in 1941, in New York.

February 16

Translation of clipping: "Our members of parliament readily deliver the funeral oration of economic liberalism. How is it that they don't see that they thus prepare their own, and that if economic liberty should die Parliament would follow it into the tomb?"

February 18

Alma-Ata is the capital of the Kazakh Soviet Socialist Republic, near the border of Chinese Turkestan. In 1928, after expulsion from the Communist Party, Trotsky, with his wife and son Leon, was banished to Alma-Ata until Trotsky's exile to Turkey a year later.

February 20

Glazman was the head of Trotsky's secretariat in Russia during the Civil War; hounded by the Communist Party leadership because of his adherence to Trotsky and the Opposition, he committed suicide in 1924. Butov, one of Trotsky's closest secretarial and staff collaborators during the Civil War, was head of the Secretariat of the Revolutionary War Committee. Arrested and imprisoned after Trotsky's expulsion from the Party, Butov refused to sign false accusations against himself, Trotsky, and the Opposition, and ended his life with a hunger strike against his treatment in prison. Blumkin, who had in 1918 assassinated the German Ambassador to Moscow, Count Wilhelm von Mirbach, as a protest against Soviet Russia's signing the Brest-Litovsk Peace Treaty imposed by the German Army, became a Communist and was employed by the Cheka, later the O.G.P.U. (see also note under April 3). A supporter of the Opposition, Blumkin was the first Russian to visit Trotsky, secretly, in exile in Turkey. Bringing back a confidential letter from Trotsky to the Opposition, Blumkin was betrayed to his superiors in the O.G.P.U.

Sermuks was chief of the military train which was Trotsky's mobile headquarters during the Civil War, and member for several years of Trotsky's secretarial staff, as was Poznansky. Expelled from the Communist Party at the same time as Trotsky, Sermuks and Poznansky followed Trotsky to banishment in Alma-Ata. There Sermuks and Poznansky were discovered by the police, who arrested them and returned them to Moscow, then deported them to he Northern wastes.

The Fourth International, as association of Trotskyist groups in various countries, was set up at Trotsky's inspiration at a congress in September, 1938, on the grounds that the Second (Socialist) International (1889) and the Third (Communist) International (1919) no longer served the needs of revolutionary socialism.

Kristian Rakovsky (1873–?), of Romanian nationality and Bulgarian descent, began his career as a revolutionary socialist in Bulgaria. After the Bolshevik Revolution, he became Chairman of the Council of People's Commissars of the Ukrainian Soviet Socialist Republic. He served for a while as Soviet Ambassador to France, but as an intimate friend and associate of Trotsky, he was expelled from the Communist Party and exiled. After renouncing his views, he was readmitted in 1934. In the Moscow Trial of

1938, however, he was charged with counterrevolutionary activities, and a sentence of twenty years' imprisonment was pronounced on him. He is believed to have died in prison.

Otto Bauer (1881–1938) was the principal theoretician of the Austrian Social Democratic Party after World War I. He succeeded Victor Adler as minister, then from 1929 to 1934 was a member of the Austrian National Council. After February, 1934, he went into exile, first in Czechoslovakia and then in France, directing from outside Austria his party's program.

March 6

In December, 1920, the congress of the French Socialist Party assembled at Tours to decide on its position on international affiliation. It was voted to affiliate with the Communist International and to take the name of the Communist Party, "S.F.I.C." (French Section of the Communist International). A minority, led by Paul Faure, Léon Blum, and others, retained the name and organization of the Socialist Party.

Jean Jaurès (1859–1914), French socialist leader, founded the newspaper, *L'Humanité*.

Marya Ilyinishna Ulyanova was the sister of Lenin (Vladimir Ilyich Ulyanov); Nadezhda Konstantinovna Krupskaya was his wife.

Trotsky's autobiography was published in translation as *My Life* (New York: Scribner's, 1930).

Paul Lafargue (1842–1911), son-in-law of Karl Marx, who, with his wife, took his own life, had been a cofounder, in 1880, of the *Parti Ouvrier Français* (French Workers' Party).

The Joint Plenum included the Party's Central Control Commission and not, as Trotsky states here, the governmental Central Executive Committee.

The "Testament," as it came to be known, was a document consisting of notes written by Lenin to the Central Committee of the

Communist Party on December 25, 1922, with a postscript added on January 4, 1923. While describing Trotsky and Stalin in the notes as "the two most able leaders of the present Central Committee," Lenin added, "Stalin is too rude and this fault, entirely supportable in relations among us Communists, becomes insupportable in the office of General Secretary. Therefore I propose to the comrades to find a way to remove Stalin from that position and oppoint to it another man who in all respects differs from Stalin only in superiority — namely, more patient, more loyal, more polite and more attentive to comrades, less capricious . . ." While it was decided after Lenin's death to suppress the "Testament," and the text has never been printed in Russia, nevertheless its authenticity was acknowledged by Stalin in 1927 and by Khrushchev in 1956.

March 10

Léon Jouhaux (1879–1954), who was awarded the Nobel Peace Prize in 1951, served as the General Secretary of the C.G.T., the national French trade-union organization, from 1909 to 1940 and from 1945 to 1947. He was the acknowledged leader of the right-wing unions in their conflict with the communist-led left-wing unions.

March 18

The Trotskys lived at Barbizon from November, 1933, to April, 1934. "Molosse" means the ancient Greek mastiff. "Benno" and "Stella" were two German shepherd dogs, a male and a female, who guarded Trotsky's house at Barbizon.

"Rudolf" was Rudolf Klement, who served as Trotsky's German-language secretary. After Trotsky's departure from France to Norway, Klement disappeared from Paris on the eve of the founding conference of the Fourth International, for which he was helping to prepare. Later, when his mutilated body was found in the Seine, his friends charged that he had been murdered by agents of the Russian secret police (G.P.U.).

March 25

G. M. Krzhizhanovsky was one of the earliest Bolshevik leaders. Camille Chautemps (1885–1963), was a leader of the Radicals, was Premier of France at the time of the Stavisky Affair, and his government was overturned in the repercussions from that scandal. Henri Dorgères was active during the thirties in organizing an extreme right-wing movement among the peasants, especially in western France. After the riots of February 6, 1934, his *Comités de Défense des Paysans de l'Ouest* merged with two other right-wing peasant groups to form the *Front Paysan.* After the formation of the Popular Front movement, Dorgères' influence dwindled.

Johann Philipp Becker, German Communist, was a leader of the Geneva section of the First International, and editor, from 1866 on, of its organ, *Vorbote*. He was a close friend of Marx and Engels. *The translation:* "You're quite right, radicalism is wearing itself away with tremendous speed. Actually there's only one more to wear out and that's Clemenceau. When his turn comes, he'll lose a whole heap of illusions, especially this: that one can rule a bourgeois republic in France these days without stealing and letting [others] steal." Georges Clemenceau (1841–1929), a Radical leader during most of his career, became premier of France and Minister of War in 1917. He earned fame as an advocate of war to the bitter end and for his role in the drafting of the Versailles Treaty.

Edouard Herriot was one of the outstanding French Radicals, and served for a time as Premier of France.

March 26

Paul-Henri Spaak (1899–1972), the present Secretary General of the North Atlantic Treaty Organization, was at that time a minister in the Belgian Cabinet.

Emile Vandervelde, like Edouard Anseele, was a leader of the Belgian socialist movement and of its parliamentary group from the end of the last century on. From 1900 to 1918 Vandervelde was president of the Bureau of the Socialist International, and was also the author of numerous works on economics, politics, and other social questions. Anseele, a member of the Belgian parliament from 1894 on, became a government minister after World War I.

"Action" is *L'Action révolutionnaire,* a paper published by the left wing of the Belgian Socialist Party.

March 27

Iskra (Spark) was a publication of Russian revolutionary Marxists, founded in 1900 by Plekhanov, Lenin, and Martov. Trotsky's first contribution to *Iskra* appeared in November, 1902.

Free translation of the Engels quotation: "There's simply no cure for that."

March 29

Henri De Man was one of the leaders of the Belgian Labor Party's right wing, and Minister of Finance in the cabinet of Prime Minister Van Zeeland. The author of many books on socialist theory, ethics, and politics, he advocated the modification and modernization of the radical views of Marx. In the thirties he moved toward a far-right political position.

"Quadragesimo Anno," an encyclical of Pope Pius XI, published on May 15, 1931, dealt with the conditions of the working classes, as did the great encyclical, "Rerum Novarum," of Pope Leo XIII, which it commemorated.

"Claude Farrère" is the pen name of Frédéric Bargone (1876–1957). Jean Louis Barthou (1862–1934), active for years in the French government, was Foreign Minister when he was assassinated, with Alexander I of Yugoslavia, by a Macedonian revolutionary at Marseilles. He had died the October before Trotsky wrote this.

"Cadets" was the popular name given to the Constitutional Democratic Party. This was Russia's principal liberal party from 1905 to 1917. The Social Revolutionists, commonly called the "SR's," formed the largest socialist movement in tsarist Russia. Anti-Marxist and populist, most of its leadership favored the peasantry and was strongly opposed to the Bolsheviks and their revolution.

By "amalgam" is meant grouping together representatives of different and even opposing political trends and accusing them of one and the same crime.

April 2

"Comintern" is an abbreviation for the Third (Communist) International.

"H. M." stands for Henri Molinier, a French adherent of Trotsky who, in his capacities as businessman and reserve army officer, was in a position to take care of tasks like arranging for Trotsky's visa to France and for his residence in that country. Molinier was killed during World War II.

April 3

"Oblomovism" takes its name from Oblomov, the hero of a book (1858–59) by Ivan Goncharov. Oblomov typifies passivity and benign inertness.

The Okhrana, like the Third Section, was the tsarist political police. After 1917, its Soviet counterparts were known successively by their abbreviated names: Cheka, O.G.P.U. (or "Gaypayoo"), N.K.V.D., M.V.D., and now K.G.B. Genrikh Yagoda, who was made chief of the O.G.P.U. by Stalin, organized and carried through the first series of purges in 1936. He was later charged with counterrevolutionary activity and sentenced to death in the Moscow Trial of 1938.

Nikolai Muralov, a Bolshevik leader under the Tsar and during the Revolution, was later head of the Moscow military district and a member of the Central Committee of the Communist Party.

Opposed to Stalin from the beginning, he was banished with Trotsky and executed for counterrevolutionary activities after the 1937 Moscow Trials.

April 4

Feliks Dzherzhinsky (1877–1926), an active Bolshevik, became the first head of the Cheka. He was aligned with Stalin against Trotsky.

Translation of newspaper clipping:

"THE U.S.S.R. WOULD PLEDGE
TO END COMMUNIST PROPAGANDA
IN GREAT BRITAIN
AND THE DOMINIONS

"London, April 3. During his recent talks with Mr. Eden, Mr. Litvinov, Soviet Commissar of Foreign Affairs, is said to have informed the Lord Privy Seal of the Moscow government's decision to end Communist propaganda in Great Britain and the Dominions.

"It appears that the funds intended for this propaganda have been progressively withdrawn during these last months."

"Fromagiste" (from *fromage* — cheese) is a French slang expression — for which the English equivalent would be "pie-card artist" — meaning a follower who supports a political machine because of the subsistence he receives from it.

April 5

Yuri Pyatakov was a Bolshevik theoretician and economist, often associated with the left wing of the Communist Party. A Trotsky supporter from 1923 to 1928, he held various government posts, and was important in the earlier Five Year Plans. He was executed after the Moscow Trial of 1937.

Aleksey Rykov (1881–1938) was a member of the Central Committee of the Communist Party for many years. A Bolshevik, he participated in the revolutions of 1905 and 1917. After Lenin's death, he was Chairman of the Council of People's Commissars. Although he supported Stalin against Trotsky, Rykov helped organize the "Right Opposition" in 1928–29, then recanted. He was sentenced to death at the 1938 Moscow Trial.

The headlines go as follows in translation:

" 'The government must forbid Red mobilization on April 7.' (*'Ami du peuple,'* April 1).

"The next day, Régnier, the RADICAL minister, obeyed.

" 'Our protest was heard.' (*'Ami du peuple,'* April 3).

"Conclusion: The government is under orders from the fascists!"

Trotsky's comment, translated: "But it isn't their final 'conclusion'; they have another: 'Let us expedite more than ever the dissolution and disarmament of fascist organizations . . .' by the government, which is under orders from the fascists!"

April 7

Translation of the newspaper clippings:

"MR. HENRI DORGÈRES CLAIMS
HE DIDN'T BREAK THE LAW
IN HIS PUBLIC TALKS

"He is moreover very confident of the outcome of the suit against him.

"Rouen, April 11. Mr. Henri Dorgères, President of the Northwest Peasants' Defense Committee, arrived this morning at Rouen and appeared before Mr. Leroy, examining magistrate.

"In the presence of Mr. Dorgères, the magistrate proceeded to break the seals and began the examination of the seized papers. Mr. Dorgères was questioned about the facts. He answered that he was ready to repeat the words he had said at public meetings, since they had contained nothing that could cause his censure.

" 'I particularly asked the peasants,' said Mr. Dorgères: ' "We may be called upon to ask you to strike against taxes. Would you be ready to answer yes?" '

"The hearing was suspended at noon and was scheduled to recommence at two o'clock, but at that time Mr. Dorgères delegated his secretary, Mr. Lefebvre, to be present at the opening of the seals because he was obliged to return to Paris, where he will take part this evening in a discussion at the Faubourg hall.

"Mr. Dorgères, whom we met as he was leaving the court, accompanied by Mr. Suplice, President of the Seine-Inférieure Peasants' Defense Committee, and by Mr. Lefebvre, Secretary General of the same committee, told us:

" 'I am not worried about the outcome of the inquiry, because nothing can be found in the seized papers or in what I said at the public meetings that could warrant prosecution.' "

"A SPEECH BY MR. HENRI DORGÈRES ON THE FRENCH PEASANTRY

"Paris, April 5. — At the Théâtre des Ambassadeurs this afternoon, Mr. Henri Dorgères gave a speech on the French peasants.

"The campaign Mr. Dorgères is waging in rural areas is well known, a campaign symbolized by his candidacy in the recent legislative election at Blois. 'The peasant will save France,' was the theme developed by the speaker as he attempted to demonstrate that the peasants represent that part of the nation which has remained sane, 'which has not, in the postwar period, known easy pleasures, parties, and the eight-hour day,' and for which he claims nothing has been done by successive governments.

"Mr. Dorgères made a defense of the peasant class and a bitter criticism of the parliamentary regime, the members of parliament, and of the government, from whom he demands reforms in the name of the corporate system and of the family."

"THE AGRICULTURAL PROGRAM OF THE PEASANT FRONT

"Tours, April 6. — At the end of a meeting this afternoon at Tours, organized by the Peasant Front, under the chairmanship of Mr. Dorgères, an order of the day was voted, stating in particular:

" 'Six thousand farmers assembled at Tours, faced by the persistent worsening of the crisis, proclaim their wish to follow a policy based on the following program:

" '1. Defense and extension of individual property, especially of small farm property;

" '2. War against excessive state socialism and fiscal charges;

" '3. War against trusts;

" '4. A solidly-built professional organization;

" '5. Revaluation of agricultural products.

" 'They ask the public authorities:

" 'a) to have an economic policy that permits all workers, including workers of the land, to live by their labors;

" 'b) to consult the representatives of agriculture whenever the interests of the profession are at stake and especially at the time of negotiations for treaties of commerce, and they protest against recent laws purporting to create more healthy conditions in the markets.' "

Colonel (Count) Casimir de la Rocque, French army officer, member of Marshal Foch's general staff between 1926 and 1928, leader of the Croix de Feu, was one of the principals in the anti-parliamentarian movement of February 6, 1934, and subsequently. The Croix de Feu, the organization he founded, was originally made up of veterans who had been decorated for service under fire. In the thirties, it became a paramilitary organization with fascist inclinations. "Badinguet" was a popular nickname in his own day for Napoleon III.

April 9

Translation of newspaper clippings:

"Danzig, April 8. — Here are the provisional official results of the election:

"The decline in Communist votes is explained chiefly by the fact that the Nazi terror has essentially been directed against the C.P. and that our Party has been reduced practically to illegality.

"The National Socialists obtained 139,043 votes, as against 109,729 on May 28 [?], 1933.

"The Social Democrats: 38,015 as against 37,882.

"The Communists: 7,990 as against 14,566.

"The Catholic Center: 31,525 as against 31,336.

"The German Nationals: 9,691 as against 13,596.

"The Poles: 8,310 as against 6,743.

"The Opposition Veterans: 382.

"Of 250,498 registered voters, of whom 13,000 come from outside the country, 234,956 valid votes were counted; that is, a proportion of about 95%, as against 92% in 1933.

"The National Socialist slate has therefore collected less than 60% of the votes and has not attained its objective of the two thirds necessary in order for it to change the Danzig constitution.

"In three months the C.G.T.U. has recruited 10,000 new adherents."

"A CANDIDATE OF FLANDIN'S BEATEN BY AN AGRARIAN IN YONNE

"In the canton of Vézelay (Yonne), the Agrarian candidate, Mary-Gallot, on Sunday was elected district councillor by 890 votes as against 648 for the Democratic Alliance candidate, Costac, who was backed by Flandin.

"The president of the council is councillor general of the same canton, and thus yesterday's results are not exactly favorable to him."

Written in the margin: "According to *Huma,* Gallot represents the 'Common Front.' "

La Vérité was the weekly newspaper of the French Trotskyist organization at this time.

The series of articles entitled "Où Va la France?" was written by Trotsky himself. In the tongue-in-cheek reference to an unknown author, Trotsky may have feared the consequences of police perusal of his papers at the time during which this diary was written. The articles appear in English openly under his name in *Whither France?* (New York: Pioneer Publishers, 1936).

Translation of the newspaper article:

"BEFORE STRESA

"KARL RADEK MAKES
A CRITICAL ANALYSIS
OF THE PROJECTED
'EUROPEAN PACT'

"Moscow, April 8. The Soviet Press is devoting long commentaries to the preparations for the Stresa conference. Among the articles published this morning, one should be mentioned in which Karl Radek makes a critical analysis of the projected pact known as 'European' which M. Laval would offer as a substitute for regional pacts.

"After having reminded readers that no decision taken at Stresa regarding the USSR will be vàlid unless the USSR is requested to approve it, Radek presents the following observations:

"1. In case of aggression in Europe it would be childish and dangerous to wait and refer the matter to the judgment of the League of Nations, as the project in preparation would seem to recommend. 'It is necessary to act,' writes Radek.

"2. The aeronautical pact anticipates an automatic and immediate sanction on the part of the Occident. Now would the danger from enemy aviation, so clearly anticipated in Western Europe, Radek continues, be any less in the East? And would the rapidity of the blow that could be aimed at the USSR be less great?

"SOME CONTRADICTIONS

"3. How can it be hoped that, in case of conflict, all the countries belonging to the League of Nations will be willing to cooperate in reestablishing security at a point in Europe where it is threatened?

"4. Is it possible to believe that Germany and Poland, who have rejected or evaded the Eastern pact by emphasizing their unwillingness to be involved in the settlement of a conflict foreign to their interests and by refusing the passage of foreign troops over their national territory, will change their point of view on the day when the universal pact replaces an Eastern pact?

"5. Finally, what effect can such a pact have when, as the British press clearly indicates, Great Britain would not participate in it?

"FOR THE EASTERN PACT

"The only result of the interminable palavers needed to pave the way for a European pact, adds Radek, will be to give those countries hostile to European order the time to complete their military preparation and to prepare an aggression.

"The spokesman concludes thus:

" 'The USSR will continue its implementation of regional pacts, grouping around it.' "

"London, April 9. — 'What a picture the satirists of the 21st century will be able to paint of our era,' exclaimed Mr. Baldwin, Lord President of the Council, during the speech he delivered yesterday evening at Llandrinod (Wales).

"The great powers appeared to him like men sick as a result of the war, sick men whose convalescence had been incessantly interrupted and arrested with setbacks. No one had wanted to submit to the major operation: disarmament. On the contrary, one remedy had been worse than the disease — economic nationalism.

"Some of them had even tried a radical medication called dictatorship. At that time crossing Europe was like walking down the corridors of a madhouse.

"In the universal upheaval, England appeared to the Lord President of the Council to be the only country that had known how to keep its balance.

" 'We haven't broken with our traditions,' he said. 'Our king is still on a throne, ruler and servant of his people; we have avoided revolution, blood, tyranny, and persecution. Our sense of humor has allowed us to give a wide berth to certain types of dreamer that have prevailed elsewhere.' "

The first headline refers to the conference at Stresa, Italy, in April, 1935. Called together by France, representatives of France, Great Britain, and Italy tried to decide what action to take as a result of Germany's formal denunciation of the Versailles Treaty articles on her disarmament.

Karl Radek (1885–?) was prominent in left-wing socialist movements in Poland, Germany, and Russia before, during, and after World War I. Returning to Russia to join the Bolsheviks after the Revolution, Radek became one of the leading members of the Presidium of the Communist International. In 1927 he was expelled from the Party, readmitted in 1930, and tried in 1937 for plotting against the Soviet Union.

April 9

On July 16, 1918, Tsar Nicholas II, the Tsarina, and all their children were shot in a cellar in Ekaterinburg, where they had been confined.

Yakov Sverdlov, one of the ablest organizers and administrators of the Bolsheviks, served as the early Soviet equivalent of Prime Minister until his death in 1919.

Poslednie Novosti (Latest News) was a newspaper published in Paris after the Bolshevik Revolution as the voice of the *émigré* "Cadets."

·

April 10

Dora Kaplan was an active member of the Socialist Revolutionary Party. In protest against the Bolshevik regime, she fired a revolver at Lenin in 1918 as he was coming out of a meeting, wounding him seriously.

April 11

Llandrindod Wells is a spa in Wales. On April 8, 1935, Sir Stanley Baldwin spoke there before the National Council of Evangelical Free Churches in support of the government White Paper on Defense, urging an increased air force to protect England against any aggressor.

April 14

Lady Cynthia was the wife of Sir Oswald Mosley, who served in the British Parliament successively as Conservative Independent and Labour member, and finally became, after World War II, the leader of the British Union of Fascists. Lady Cynthia's father, Lord Curzon, had been Governor General of India, and later a member of the War Committee of the wartime British cabinet. From that time on, he was active in British foreign relations. The "I.L.P." of Lady Cynthia's letter is the Independent Labour Party, one of the oldest socialist organizations in Great Britain. It was partly responsible for the creation of the Labour Party, in which it long formed the left wing. Although it later withdrew and was on some issues close to the Trotskyists in the late 1930's, most of its leaders remained with or returned to the Labour Party.

April 29

Translation of the clippings:

"We have accomplished our revolution; we have even waited more than half a century to reap its benefits. Today we possess the necessary frameworks for every possible reform, for every development, for every kind of progress."

"We could then agree neither with those who refer to the revolutionary action nor to those who deny the necessity for organizing the national defense according to its needs."

"THE POPE BLESSES THE FAITHFUL AT LOURDES BY RADIO.

"Lourdes, April 28. — The pontifical mass ended today at 4:20 P.M.

"A little later, loudspeakers announced that Vatican City would be heard and that His Holiness Pius XI would give his blessing to the faithful. Then, several minutes later, amid the most profound silence, Pius XI offered to the crowd his thanks and gratitude for having come from all parts of the world in such large numbers."

May 2

Dr. Martin was a local political leader in Grenoble.

May 4

Aleksandr Potemkin was at this time Soviet Ambassador to France.

May 5

Max Eastman (1883–1969) was editor of *The Masses* before World War I, then editor of *The Liberator*. From 1923 on, he supported the Trotsky Opposition for a number of years, and became

Trotsky's translator and literary representative in the United States. Author of books criticizing the Stalin regime and proposing a revision of Marx's theories along more revolutionary lines, he later renounced socialism.

Sergo Orzhonikidze, who had been active in Georgian and Russian revolutionary movements under the Tsar, was a member of the Bolshevik Party and was also active during the Revolution and Civil War. A close personal friend of Stalin, and his supporter in all internal party disputes, Orzhonikidze held several important posts.

May 8

The expression "last ditch" originated in the sentence, "France is the last ditch of freedom in Europe," made famous by Edouard Daladier.

"M" refers to Raymond Molinier, brother of "H.M." (Henri Molinier), mentioned on April 2. The "young French comrade" is Jean van Heijenoort, who served from 1932 to 1939 as Trotsky's secretary in Turkey, France, Norway, and Mexico. "G." was Inspecteur Gagneux of the *Sûreté nationale*.

Léon Daudet, the son of Alphonse Daudet, was an ultranationalistic journalist and literary critic, much of whose work appeared in the royalist newspaper, *L'Action française*. He was one of the inspirers of the royalist organization, Camelots du Roi. Charles Maurras, who strongly influenced him, was associated with him on *L'Action française* and in the "Camelots."

May 9

Unser Wort was a German Trotskyist publication whose name was derived from the title (*Nashe Slovo*) of the Russian newspaper published in Paris during World War I by Trotsky and his colleagues.

May 10

The "Basel congress" was an international congress of socialists, held on November 24, 1912, to confer about the best means of preventing war in Europe. The French socialists and the Germans and Austrians found themselves sharply divided on the resolution of which Trotsky speaks, which was against war, eloquently written but without any specific suggestions as to how to prevent it.

May 13

Marshal Jozef Pilsudski (1867–1935), Poland's chief of state after World War I, had been a leader of the nationalist revolutionary wing of the Polish socialist movement; he founded the Polish Socialist Party.

Translation of the letter:

"Brussels, May 9, 1935

"Comrade L. D.

"Here are some details of the meeting of the B.E. of the I.O.S.

"1. Attached you will find the resolution as it came out of the Committee. I have made changes in it according to the text that appeared in the newspapers.

"2. Vandervelde is no longer a member of the B.E. The statutes do not allow him to be a minister and a member of the committee at the same time. But he is present at each meeting of the secretariat. He has even suggested meeting in his ministerial office. Adler was opposed to this.

"3. He was likewise present at the first meeting of the Executive Committee. The minutes cannot mention it.

"4. Breitscheid came to visit his friends but was not present at the meeting.

"5. The press does not mention the names of the Austrian delegates. They were Bauer and Pollak. Ditto for the one from Czechoslovakia; it was Leo de Winter.

"6. Not a word about the III International.

"7. The whole session was taken up in working out the definitive resolution, of which Blum's was the point of departure.

"8. We spent five minutes in setting up a committee which would function . . . in wartime. It was Dan who made this proposal. After the meeting Blum went up to ask him (making fun of him) whether he was the true author of the proposal. Dan replied that that was a proposal of the Polish socialists.
"9. For two days we discussed this resolution. The person who quibbled the most was the English delegate. Our comrade had the impression that he (William Gillis; the others were silent) felt he had full responsibility for the Labour Party. The others seemed rather to be acting on their own behalf.
"10. The Italian delegate was also more or less opposed. He flatly wanted the resolution to mention the imperialistic plan of Italian Fascism in Africa. After his intervention the amendment underlined by me in the text was added. This no doubt so that he can explain himself to his section. The others flatly did not want the name of Abyssinia to figure in the text.

"Our comrade, since he could not be present at all the sections, could not get better information.

Communist greetings,
G. Ver."

"I.O.S." stands for "International Ouvrière et Socialiste" (the Labor and Socialist — Second — International); "B.E." stands for "Bureau Exécutif" (Executive Bureau).

For Vandervelde, see note under March 26. Friedrich Adler, son of Victor Adler, was the socialist pacifist who in 1916 assassinated Count Stürgkh, the Austrian Prime Minister. At the time of this meeting, Friedrich Adler was Secretary of the International.

Rudolf Breitscheid, an economist specializing in finance, was a leader of the German Social Democratic Party during the Weimar Republic, which he served as a cabinet minister. Otto Bauer is mentioned in the Notes for February 18. Oskar Pollak was one of the leaders of the Austrian Social Democratic Party, then in exile. "Leo de Winter" was Lev Winter, the first Minister of Social Welfare in Czechoslovakia. He is remembered for his efforts to introduce legislation for social insurance and for his collaboration in writing a handbook of industrial law. Fedor (Theodore) Dan was one of the leaders of the Russian Social Democratic — or Menshevik — Party in exile. William Gillis was then representative of the British Labour Party to the Executive Bureau of the International.

May 14

Aleksandr Ulyanov, Lenin's older brother, was a revolutionary agrarian socialist, or Populist (*"Narodnik"*). In 1887, Ulyanov was tried and executed for an attempt on the life of Tsar Alexander III.

Egor Lazarev, son of Russian peasants, was another Populist revolutionary. He lived abroad for many years, helped to form the neopopulist Russian Social Revolutionist Party, and in 1917 was one of its right-wing leaders. Vera Figner (1852–1942), a Russian doctor, was one of the founders of the early populist "Land and Liberty" movement. Later she became a member of the terrorist "People's Will." After the movement was responsible for the assassination of Alexander II in 1881, she was the only member not captured by the police. Finally caught, imprisoned, and exiled, she did not return to Russia until 1916. After being chairman of a committee to assist political prisoners, she retired to write her memoirs.

May 15

Translation of letter:

"Extracts from a dialogue.

"C. Don't you think that T's desire to move springs from his difficulties with his landlord?

"H. Difficulties? Do you believe that he has difficulties there?

"C. Of course: Oh, the old boy is probably not very agreeable, you know; it's only with us that it does not go! (Smiles . . .)

"H. 'Difficulties' seems to me an awfully big word; it's true I may have sensed a few little misunderstandings, but I've never heard any talk of difficulties . . .

"I think that your 'informants' have quite exaggerated things so that they could have a good 'report.'

"C. Don't be misled, it's a friend who let me know the thing accidentally, and not at all with a bad intention, since he does not wish any harm to Mr. Trotsky, and, on the contrary, was quite annoyed by the result . . .

"H. I think that you've been fooled —

"C. I don't think so at all; anyway we would prefer that it not be true, because it will be enough trouble for us if his landlord makes him move, we are not interested in having this thing start up again.

"H. I ought to tell you that I made a little inquiry about the trip, that you told me about, of his son in the East. The person in question demonstrated to me that he did not travel at all! Your agents must have mixed him up with some friend or other of T's.

"C. I don't think so; our information is excellent.

"H. The police always believes its information to be excellent, but it gets biased information too often to have the right to claim that. The young man is preparing for three certificates at the Sorbonne, etc., etc., etc. . . .

"C. I know it well, and besides if it is not he who made the trip it comes to the same thing (gestures and smiles).

"H. I don't understand!

"C. We have our information on his political activity; it seems that for some months he has been working and staying put — that's better, it's exact . . .

"Then discussion of no interest about the police — their information — with a statement that the Russian police have a simple task because in that country everybody has a mania of informing and self-accusation . . . etc. (Commonplaces). Then, confidence in the outcome of national elections before the German peril — the Germans, these unassimilable people whom we know so well — all these refugees, we remain enemies for them; they will take up their guns again at the first call.

"As you see, relations are most cordial . . . but where T. is concerned, all depends on the minister who decides 'this question' himself. (I believe that's true.)"

May 16

"Wittels' book about Freud" is: Fritz Wittels, *Sigmund Freud; His Personality, His Teaching, and His School,* trans. (New York: Dodd, Mead, 1924).

May 17

Translation of the first clipping:

"They were wholly in agreement about recognizing, in the present state of the international situation, the obligations that force themselves upon the governments sincerely dedicated to safeguarding the peace and which have clearly demonstrated this desire for peace by their participation in every search for mutual guarantees, precisely in the interest of preserving peace. Duty first of all obligates them not to weaken in any way their means of national defense. In this respect Mr. Stalin understands and fully approves of the policy of national defense made by France in order to keep its armed strength at the level of security."

August 4, 1914, was the date on which the Social Democratic Party fraction in the German Reichstag voted to support the war and to grant war credits to the government. To left-wing socialist opponents of this action, which was followed substantially by the French, British, Belgian, and Austrian socialists in their respective parliaments, the fourth of August became the symbol of the betrayal, by the right-wing and moderate socialists, who predominated in the Socialist International, of international socialist principles.

Translation of the second clipping:

"IN THE NEWSPAPERS

"WILL THE FRENCH COMMUNISTS OBEY STALIN?

"As we know, the final communiqué issued at the close of Mr. Laval's conferences with Stalin, Litvinov, and Molotov 'fully approves of the policy of national defense made by France to keep its armed strength at the level of security.'

"A reprinting of the comments on this subject made by the newspapers of the common front is not without interest. It will be seen that the explanations in *L'Humanité* explain nothing and that, in the last analysis, the French Communists, in great embarrassment, remain opposed to the French army.

"L'HUMANITÉ (Mr. Magnien):

"Stalin has properly said that he approves of the defense measures taken against the forces of Hitler.

"Where can the danger of agression come from? From Hitler's fascism, which refuses to participate in any plan for peace, which increases its efforts against Memel, Austria, etc.

"Mutual assurance implies appropriate measures for the defense of the peace. Moreover, the peace policy of the Soviet Union, oriented towards the interests of the worker masses of the U.S.S.R. and of all other countries, constantly leads to disarmament. The collective organization of peace postulates disarmament, because once security has been assured to all, the conditions of simultaneous and general disarmament will be assured as well.

"As for us French Communists, our line of action hasn't changed. The U.S.S.R. treats with bourgeois governments because it is surrounded by bourgeois governments. But the workers know well they can't trust their bourgeoisie to defend the peace.

"The French Communists, the French workers, can't have confidence in the leaders of the army of the French bourgeoisie. There are many fascists among Weygand's officers, Croix de Feu men and French Hitlerites. All the acts of the French fascists — which the French government covers up — prove that their sympathies are with Hitler and with German fascism, the main fomentor of war in Europe.

"The French Communists and workers, who are leading the bitter fight against fascism, know that these men are ready to betray the Franco-Soviet pact in order to ally themselves with Hitler against the U.S.S.R. The force France can place in the service of defending the peace can only be a sure force under the dominion of the action of the worker masses fighting ceaselessly against fascism and the bourgeoisie to chase the reactionary and fascist officers from the army.

"We shall do everything possible to defend the peace and the rampart of peace, the Soviet Union. That's why we shall continue to do everything possible to combat the internal enemies of peace and the U.S.S.R., to fight against the chauvinistic alarms that are just the opposite of the defense of peace and that precipitate war.

"Everything for the defense of liberty and peace, everything for the defense of the U.S.S.R., for the support of its strong peace policy. Everything so that socialism, triumphant over a sixth of the globe, may be victorious over the fascism in the world. That is the struggle for peace the Communists are engaged in.

"LE POPULAIRE (Léon Blum):

"Stalin sides against us and with the government we have fought; that government's representative at Moscow will return armed with his certificate of good conduct.

"He sides against us and with the adversaries from whom we have just suffered a blow in the recent electoral battle.

"The position of us socialists, who, without denying the necessity of defending French soil against invasion, nevertheless refuse to join in the military concepts and organization of the bourgeoisie — our position is the object of condemnation.

"This condemnation is implicit; but it is evident.

"I fear that Stalin has not, from Moscow, measured the repercussion his words have on the political situation in France and on the proletarian situation in France.

"LE PEUPLE (organ of the C.G.T.):

"We must realize that Mr. Laval has been demanding and that Stalin completely disregards the French Communist Party. Because today that party is in a frankly ridiculous position.

"We shall see if the Communists are free men or if their dependency with regard to Moscow is as complete as we have always said it was. For our part, we believe they are going to bow low before Stalin's ukase. Already their campaign against the two years [of military service?] has been radically halted.

"Thus, today, Mussolini, Weygand, Laval, and Stalin are in agreement in publicly affirming that the security of a nation rests, first of all, on the quality of its army. It is in the name of this revolutionary policy that, one of these days, the French proletarians will be asked to put on uniforms for the common defense of the French bourgeoisie and the Russian bureaucracy.

"But *will* the French proletarians, and especially the French Communists, march on behalf of this policy? Will they allow someone to scoff at them so shamelessly, with such characteristic ease?

"Here also are two other comments:

"LE TEMPS:

"In opposition to the revolutionary dictator of Moscow, the symbol and living incarnation of the Russian Communist Party and of international Communism, the Socialist Party rises as the champion of defeatism; for defeatism also consists in opposing methods recognized as indispensable for insuring national defense and maintaining the armed forces at a level of security. It remains to be seen whether the Radical Party can, from now on, tolerate the least contact with socialist defeatism, with the opposite of patriotism. Throwing a monkey-wrench into the Marxist frog-puddle is also throwing a monkey-wrench into the cartel fish-pond . . .

"PARIS-MIDI (Marcel Lucain):

"Let us recognize without passion and with complete impartiality that Stalin has just made the job very difficult for the revolutionaries of this country. France, to be sure, had no need of the approval of a foreign leader, even of the Soviet dictator, in order to know its rights and its need for security. But no one is deceived about the exclusive objective of this communiqué that is essentially aimed at disavowing antimilitarism and inflicting on Blum and Cachin a contradiction so sharp, in the eyes of the world, that the common front will be left speechless by it. This intention has also demonstrated a little something about the unusual nature of such an interference by the leader of Bolshevism in our most secret affairs: a friendship, especially when new, with the warmth of the initial contacts, may explain certain audacities. Nevertheless, Mr. Blum is at once hurt and indignant."

May 23

"Jeanne" is Jeanne Martin Despallières, the wife of Trotsky's son Leon (Lyova).

Translation of note — the French of the original has not been corrected:

"I am happy to let you know that the board of directors voted unanimously to give the authorization in question. It remains only to complete the formalities. In 2 or two and a half days (perhaps 3) we shall have the text which we shall forward immediately to Crux (for signing). At that time Crux will also receive all the particulars of the transaction." "Crux" was one of the pseudonyms used by Trotsky.

June 1

"Komsomol" is the abbreviation for the youth organization of the U.S.S.R. Kurt Rosenfeld was a German lawyer, member of the left wing of the Social Democratic Party, then of the more radical "S.A.P." (Socialist Workers' Party).

June 6

France was undergoing a financial crisis at this time. In May, the cabinet had demanded almost dictatorial powers in order to save the franc, and had been overthrown. Late in July, the new government was given emergency financial powers, and began retrenchment.

June 8

"L.S." cannot be further identified. Her father, Semyon Lvovich Kliachko, lived for years in Vienna, where he died in 1914. He became the Trotskys' most intimate friend during their second exile under the tsarist regime.

Avvakum (1620?–1681) was twice exiled for his doctrines and was finally burned at the stake. In 1673, he wrote his autobiography, which was remarkable partly for being in vernacular Russian. The book was extremely popular with schismatics in the Russian Orthodox Church.

June 9

"Van" is Jean van Heijenoort, referred to on May 8.

"Professor Piccard (the Belgian)" probably means the Swiss physicist and aeronaut, Auguste Piccard (1844–1962), who had succeeded in 1932 in a record-setting balloon ascent, financed by the Belgian government.

June 20

In the first years of the Russian Revolution, André Marty led a mutiny of sailors aboard French warships engaged in military intervention against Soviet Russia. Under Stalin, he rose to important positions in the Communist International and the French Communist Party. For a while member of the Chamber of Deputies, he was expelled from the French Communist Party after World War II.

"Dr. R." is Dr. Rosenthal, a Paris physician. His son Gérard was at that time a member of the French Trotskyist group.

Olaf Scheflo, one of the leaders of the Norwegian Labor Party, was spokesman for the left wing during World War I and an advocate of affiliation with the Communist International. A few years later, the party withdrew from the International and remained without international affiliation until it entered the Socialist International. While Trotsky was writing this, Scheflo was editor of a party newspaper in Christiansund.

At the national congress of the French Socialist Party in Mulhouse, France, the Trotskyists (who had only recently entered the Party) challenged the policy of the leadership, putting forward the program advocated by Trotsky.

Walter Held was a German Trotskyist who had fled to Norway when Hitler came to power.

"Rous" is Jean Rous, who joined the French Trotskyist movement in the thirties.

Jan Frankel, a Czechoslovakian Trotskyist, served Trotsky as secretary in Turkey, Norway, and Mexico.

The Storting is the Norwegian parliament.

Translation of the typewritten page:

"The working class of the nation and all right-thinking unprejudiced people, moreover, will welcome the government's decision. The right of asylum must be no dead letter but a reality. Therefore the Norwegian people does not feel itself insulted — like Höire (the conservatives) — but honored by Trotsky's stay here in this country.

"The Norwegian workers and their party take no position on his politics. For we do not have the requisite information to form a solid opinion about what has come between Stalin and Trotsky. It is possible that Stalin has judged the situation more correctly, in terms of political realities, than his rival. But that does not justify the victorious faction in harassing a man like Leo Trotsky and banishing him from his country — Trotsky whose name will stand beside Lenin's in the history of the Russian Revolution. If, despite his great and indisputable services, he is banished from his country, every democratic people must regard it a duty of love to give him shelter, especially since he is ill and broken down and needs a period of convalescence."

Martin Tranmael was a leader of the Norwegian Labor Party and editor of its central newspaper, *Arbeiderbladet,* in Oslo. Tranmael was a Communist when the Norwegian party was affiliated with the Communist International. After resisting the demands of the Executive Committee of the International for expelling dissident elements, he broke completely with the International. Later, he helped bring the Norwegian Labor Party into affiliation with the Socialist International.

Avely Enukidze, a Georgian revolutionist, was Stalin's intimate friend and one of the oldest members of the Bolshevik Party. For years a member of the party's Central Committee and Secretary of the Central Executive Committee of the Soviet Union, he was expelled from the party in 1935 for "political and moral dissoluteness," after being suspected by Stalin of helping political prisoners and exiles of the Opposition. He was executed in 1937 after trial for "espionage and terroristic activities."

Mikhail Kalinin (1875–1946), a factory worker who had been active in the Social Democratic Party under tsarism, was elected in 1919 a member of the party's Central Committee and Chairman of the Executive Committee of the Soviet Government. From 1938 to 1946, Kalinin headed the Presidium of the Supreme Soviet of the U.S.S.R.

June 24

Le Matin was an important conservative daily newspaper, published in Paris.

June 26

Arkhangelskoe is a village some forty miles from Moscow. When they were living in the Kremlin, Trotsky and his wife used to go to Arkhangelskoe at times to rest.

June 29

The *Aftenposten* is a conservative daily newspaper published in Oslo.

July 1

Emma Goldman (1869–1940) was a Russian-born anarchist, who came to the United States at the age of seventeen and was deported in 1919. She went to Russia, but was disillusioned by the conflict between her ideals and the actualities of the Soviet regime. After traveling to England, she settled in Canada.

"Mother" Jones was a militant labor agitator and organizer in the United States, especially in the coal-mining areas of Pennsylvania and West Virginia and in the ore-mining regions of the West and Southwest. She was still active in the labor movement after she was ninety (*The Autobiography of Mother Jones* [Chicago: Charles H. Kerr Co., 1925]).

Prince Peter Kropotkin (1842–1921) was a distinguished Russian geographer who became a revolutionary early in life. He embraced anarchism in the 1870's, and became a socialist leader later in that decade.

Konrad Knudsen, after being an I.W.W. member in the United States, returned to his native Norway to become active in the Norwegian Labor Party and in the parliament. Trotsky lived, during his stay in Norway, in Knudsen's home in Weksal, a village near Oslo.

July 30

Trygve Lie (1896–1968), was at that time a Labor Party leader.

September 8.

The Torgsin was an official Soviet trading organization before World War II, handling the sale of goods to Russians on the basis of contributions sent from abroad.

Platon Volkov's reference to "the road of the old Lafargues" and "almost joining our Zinushka" is to the fact that the Lafargues and Volkov's wife, Trotsky's daughter Zinaida, all died by suicide. "Grandmother," is Sokolovskaya, author of the preceding letter.

Index

INDEX